Good News About Jesus Christ

12 Life-Changing Personal
or Bible Group Studies

Good News About Jesus Christ

12 Life-Changing Personal or Bible Group Studies

Editor

MELVIN E. BANKS, LITT.D.

Based on selected New Testament Scriptures

Urban Ministries, Inc.

Copyright © 2020 by Melvin E. Banks, LITT.D.
All rights reserved.

First printing 1989; second printing 1993; third printing 1994; fourth printing 1998.

No part of this book may be reproduced or transmitted in any form or by any means, electronic or mechanical, including photocopying, recording, video, or by any information or retrieval system, without prior written permission from the publisher except for the use of brief quotations in a book review.

Our thanks to the following persons for their contributions to the writing of Bible studies contained in this volume: Bennie Goodwin, (Ph.D.), Philip Rodman, (M.A.), Reverend Walter McCray, Fred Thomas, and Dr. A. Okechukwu Ogbonnaya, (Ph.D).

Published in the United States by Urban Ministries, Inc.
P. O. Box 436987
Chicago, IL 60643
www.urbanministries.com 1-800-860-8642

ISBN 978-0-940955-49-3 (paperback)
ISBN 978-1-68353-668-0 (eBook)

Unless otherwise noted, scripture texts are taken from the King James Version of the Bible. Other versions quoted include the following:

LB—Living Bible, c. 1971
NIV—New International Version, c. 1973, 1978, 1984
RSV—The Revised Standard Version, c. 1952, 1971.

Cover design by Laura Duffy Design
Book design by Amit Dey

Printed in the United States of America.

This book is dedicated to Olive Banks, my devoted wife of many years. She has been a great encouragement to me as through the years we have worked together in the development of UMI. This book is also dedicated to Regis Scott Banks, my eldest grandson, whose intelligence and sense of humor are my inspiration.

TABLE OF CONTENTS

Preface ix
Foreword xv
Introduction xvii
Bible Study Guides
  1. Who Jesus Is 1
  2. Yielding to God's Will 15
  3. Born a Saviour 26
  4. Coping With Doubts and Fears 39
  5. Do As I Have Done 53
  6. Teaching About Priorities 63
  7. Reversing the World's Standard 81
  8. Forgiveness 104
  9. The Gospel Has No Boundaries 122
  10. Citizens of Two Kingdoms 141
  11. The Lord's Supper 167
  12. Working for Reconciliation 186
About the Author 207

Preface

How To Use This Book

The materials in these studies provide for in-depth exploration of the Scriptures. At the same time, we recognize that merely studying Bible texts as an end in itself is not adequate to accomplish all that should be accomplished.

The Scriptures make clear that God's purpose for people is that first they would come to know Him as Saviour (2 Peter 3:9), then go on to develop their relationship with Him so their lifestyles increasingly reflect the character of Jesus Christ (1 Peter 2:2).

We read in Romans 8:29 that God "predestinated [us] to be conformed to the image of His Son." In other words, God's desires for believers is that they become more and more like Jesus Christ in character. We know that Jesus Christ is perfect and that we will never reach ultimate perfection in this lifetime. At the same time, we are encouraged to pursue the likeness of Christ. Note the purpose of each of the following sections which appear throughout the studies:

- DEFINING THE ISSUE
- AIM
- SCRIPTURE TEXT
- BIBLE BACKGROUND

- POINTS TO PONDER
- LESSON AT-A-GLANCE
- EXPLORING THE MEANING
- DISCERNING MY DUTY
- DECIDING MY RESPONSE
- LIGHT ON THE HEAVY
- MORE LIGHT ON THE TEXT

DEFINING THE ISSUE

These studies are designed to help people grow in their relationship with Jesus Christ, to foster discipleship. Each study begins with a section we call "DEFINING THE ISSUE." The purpose of this is to elevate a life need which will be addressed in the exploration of the Scripture text.

Scholars have observed that every book in the Bible was written to address a life need which the people to whom the book is addressed were experiencing—whether to document their history, deal with a false doctrine, or encourage holiness of life.

AIM

This is a statement of what the study is designed to accomplish in the life of the participant. Such aims can be modified to address the needs which the leader of the group senses to be those of the group. A leader should never feel that the written aim has to be slavishly adhered to. The study is a "guide," not an unchangeable focus.

SCRIPTURE TEXT

This section includes a printed portion of Scripture upon which the study focuses. While the studies were prepared using the King

James Version of the Bible, any version that the group prefers can be used. This section begins with an outline of the text which facilitates dividing the Scripture into smaller segments.

BIBLE BACKGROUND

This section provides contextual material which can aid in understanding the people to whom the Scripture was originally addressed. It also explains the context for the Scripture portion, so the text is easier to grasp.

POINTS TO PONDER

These questions are designed to help focus the minds of participants on some of the areas the study will address and to facilitate understanding the text.

LESSON AT-A-GLANCE

This section is an outline of the text which facilitates dividing the Scripture into smaller segments.

EXPLORING THE MEANING

Comments on the Scripture texts will be found in this section. If at all possible, participants will have read this material prior to the gathering so that reading entire sections is not necessary. However, the leader may want portions to be read in order to reinforce a particular point of discussion.

DISCERNING MY DUTY

Since the discussion of meaning should not be an end in itself, we have provided a section entitled, "DISCERNING MY DUTY." While in many cases this allows the participant to think about individual responses to the Scripture, occasionally this exercise may focus on group action. This is especially helpful if you think of your group as more than a "study" group. For example, your people will occasionally want to collectively engage in some activity which reinforces the aim of the study as well as promote the welfare of others.

DECIDING MY RESPONSE

Since there is a difference between knowing what could be done and actually doing it, "DECIDING MY RESPONSE" allows a participant to pinpoint what their response will be as a result of discovering what could be done.

LIGHT ON THE HEAVY

This section will provide additional information on a word or theme which may be helpful to the readers.

MORE LIGHT ON THE TEXT

When this section appears, it represents additional insights on the text which further illuminate the text for the reader.

OTHER SUGGESTIONS

1. As a way of strengthening the bonds among people within your group, you may want to plan some kind of social event once per quarter. This may consist of a potluck supper, a dinner/outing, etc.
2. You may want to consider some form of ministry activity during the course of a study, such as one of the following:
    - Conduct a jail or prison service.
    - Make or purchase gifts for a public or private school class.

- Organize a special church cleaning.
- Conduct a fundraising project for a missionary.
- Gather clothing for needy children.
- Write letters to a politician on a local or national issue of morality or justice.
- Organize a fundraiser to send a needy child to a summer camp or vacation.

  A little time spent brainstorming in your group will produce lots of other ideas for serving the Lord and people in a practical way.

3. You may want to use a portion of your time to allow your group members to pray for one another and for the needs of the church.

Foreword

CELEBRATE 50 YEARS WITH US!

When UMI began in 1970, African Americans were still struggling to undo the effects of 350 years of slavery and Jim Crow segregation.

We believed both then and now that the more we know and rely on God's revelation in the Bible, the more we will be equipped to serve Him and to deal with racism, injustice, and to represent Jesus Christ in our world.

Three books, *The Unfolding Story of God's Salvation Plan*, *God Delivers on His Promise*, and *Good News about Jesus Christ*, are examples of UMI Bible studies that enrich our knowledge of God's Word. In these and other Bible studies, we explore not only our need for personal holiness but also God's standards for social justice and righteous living.

Since 1970, life has improved for many African Americans. Yes, we have a long way to go, but we see progress. Many churches have enriched their Christian educational programs. Surveys show that today a high number of young adults cling to the church and the Christian faith to help them cope with injustice and to live right. UMI's approach in presenting biblical truth improves total growth by offering Bible studies contextualized and professionally produced for African American children, youth, and adults.

It gives me great joy to see how God is using these materials to transform people for His eternal purposes.

It is clear that the mode of teaching is changing from analog to digital. This rapid change challenges churches to upgrade communication methods to accommodate digitized content. We know God's truth will never change because God is eternal truth. Still, our ways of teaching must adjust to a changing culture. For the 50th anniversary edition, these three books, which were originally published in print only, are now available as eBooks. We hope to see millions of more people come to love and live for our Lord in the years ahead.

African Americans are conscious of our African roots, and we seek to connect with brothers and sisters on the continent and in the African diaspora. Together, we can have a greater impact on the world for Christ and His eternal kingdom.

Carl Jeffrey Wright
Chief Executive Officer
Urban Ministries, Inc.
Chicago, Illinois
September 8, 2020

Introduction

The studies in this book highlight certain significant events in the life of Jesus Christ and of the Church following its establishment at Pentecost. The purpose of these selected studies is to give an overview of the New Testament in 12 studies under the theme of "Good News About Jesus Christ."

The first four lessons confirm that the Good News is that Jesus came into the world to save sinners. The good news did not just happen at Calvary, but began even before Jesus was born in Bethlehem. It is good news that Jesus was born of a woman. The situation surrounding His birth was extraordinary. His birth was announced by an angel of God. His mother was a young woman who would not have been chosen by the human rulers of the time. Though young and poor, God chose Mary. At His birth, Jesus was good news to His mother. He was good news to the shepherds in the field. He was good news to the wise men who came from an ancient land. Heaven saw His birth as good news. The angels who sang on the eve saw it as good news. His life was good news to the sick whom He offered healing. It was good news to those whose dead bodies He brought back to life with a gentle touch of the hand. His life was good news to those whose lives He snatched from the clutches of demonic oppression by the power of the spoken Word. His death, though tragic, embodied for us the extent to which God will go to show how much He cares for this world.

His resurrection is good news because it offers insight into the fact that death is not the ultimate victor. In Him, God offers a way to eternal life in the presence of God. This is Good News.

Beginning with lesson five, four important teachings of Jesus are the focus of study: love, greed, true greatness, and forgiveness. Each lesson reveals that Jesus' teachings are different from the values that the world teaches. LOVE: The good news is that God is love and God's love is revealed in the person of Jesus. This same love is manifested in the lives of those who truly follow the Lord Jesus Christ. In fact, love is what shows the difference between those who know Jesus Christ and those who do not know Him. GREED: Greed is one of the destructive sicknesses of our age and the lesson for this topic is designed to teach us how to deal with greed. TRUE GREATNESS: We are taught that true greatness is not attained by the material things that we have, but by our willingness to serve and our commitment to God. FORGIVENESS: Forgiveness is a principle which allows us to live out the good news of Jesus in our lives.

In the final five lessons, we lift up passages of Scripture that tell how the faithful can live in accordance with the teachings of Jesus in a world that is at odds with the message of the Gospel. The realization that the world is at odds with the Gospel is obvious to anyone who desires to share the good news with the world. The world does not desire to remain steadfast with God. Instead it seeks to impose its own standard on God. By attempting to impose its own standard on God rather than following God's revelation, the world is always at odds with divine revelation. In these lessons, we see how the faith of the first-century Christians helped them to face internal strife and external pressures. We shall also see how this faith enabled them, through the process of expansion and change, to fulfill their mission of reconciliation.

Who Jesus Is
Based on Matthew 16:13-23

DEFINING THE ISSUE

Richard Wright wrote a short story about a young boy who painted Jesus black (see *Uncle Tom's Children*, 1938). Today this would not be as big an issue as it was in 1938. This young boy's painting was done at a time when a picture of a Black Christ was not at all acceptable. In the story, the Black principal at the boy's school failed to get a major promotion because he dared to place the painting in a school-wide competition. His white supervisor exploded with anger. He could not understand why the principal commended the child instead of reprimanding him.

Even today, controversy continues about the color of Jesus Christ. A study of geography, anthropology, and the Bible leads to the conclusion that Jesus was not the white person so typically portrayed in most Bible art. And this affirmation is especially important to young people of African descent. However, the question Christ wants us to clarify in our minds and hearts is not how He looks, but who He is. How we personally identify Him is much more important than how we depict Him. Peter helps us make an intelligent identification of the Master.

AIM

By the end of the lesson, students will explore Peter's declaration of Christ's divine identity, become convinced of the accuracy of Peter's affirmation, determine to give Christ the honor such an affirmation deserves, and communicate this truth to others.

SCRIPTURE TEXT

> MATTHEW 16:13 When Jesus came into the coasts of Caesarea Philippi, he asked his disciples, saying, Whom do men say that I the Son of man am?
>
> 14 And they said, Some say that thou art John the Baptist: some, Elias; and others, Jeremias, or one of the prophets.
>
> 15 He saith unto them, But whom say ye that I am?
>
> 16 And Simon Peter answered and said, Thou art the Christ, the Son of the living God.
>
> 17 And Jesus answered and said unto him, Blessed art thou, Simon Barjona: for flesh and blood hath not revealed it unto thee, but my Father which is in heaven.
>
> 18 And I say also unto thee, That thou art Peter, and upon this rock I will build my church; and the gates of hell shall not prevail against it.
>
> 19 And I will give unto thee the keys of the kingdom of heaven: and whatsoever thou shalt bind on earth shall be bound in heaven: and whatsoever thou shalt loose on earth shall be loosed in heaven.
>
> 20 Then charged he his disciples that they should tell no man that he was Jesus the Christ.

21 From that time forth began Jesus to show unto his disciples, how that he must go unto Jerusalem, and suffer many things of the elders and chief priests and scribes, and be killed, and be raised again the third day.

22 Then Peter took him, and began to rebuke him, saying, Be it far from thee, Lord: this shall not be unto thee.

23 But he turned, and said unto Peter, Get thee behind me, Satan: thou art an offence unto me: for thou savourest not the things that be of God, but those that be of men.

BIBLE BACKGROUND

Before Jesus came to earth, the Jews had a definite idea of the Messiah and what He would accomplish. According to the Prophet Isaiah, the long-awaited Messiah would occupy the earthly throne of King David. The prophet wrote, "He will reign on David's throne and over his kingdom, establishing and upholding it with justice and righteousness from that time on and forever" (Isaiah 9:7, NIV). The scribes of Jesus' day had completely overlooked Isaiah's assertion that God's Servant, the Messiah, would suffer and die (Isaiah 53).

During Peter's time, Israel was ruled by Herod the Great, a usurper to the throne and a puppet of Rome. The people believed the Messiah would assume the throne of David and overthrow the Roman oppressors. He would restore Israel to her past glory. Many of those who accepted Jesus as Messiah expected Him to establish His throne at that time.

Peter, the main character in the text for this study, was introduced to Jesus by his brother Andrew (John 1:40, 41). Andrew had listened to Jesus' teaching and believed Him to be the Messiah. Andrew immediately went and found Simon Peter, telling him, "We have found the Messiah" (1:41, NIV). He took Peter to meet Christ and Peter also believed. Later, by the Sea of Galilee, Christ approached the brothers about a total commitment. Peter and Andrew were tending to their fishing enterprise when Jesus said to them, "Follow me, and I will make you fishers of men" (Matthew 4:19). Jesus needed a group of men in His ministry that would travel with Him, learn from Him, and be able to carry on His ministry once He left earth. Peter and Andrew responded immediately to Jesus' call. They left their business and followed Him (v. 20).

POINTS TO PONDER

1. *Describe the geographical setting where Jesus chose to question His disciples about His identity. (v. 13)*

2. *What was Jesus' first question to them? (v. 13)*

3. *How did the disciples answer this question? (v. 14) The people they thought Jesus might be were all dead. What does this reveal about the Jews' belief about people returning to life? Did they have a correct understanding about life after death?*

4. *Jesus' second question was more focused on the disciples' opinion of Him. Why did Jesus want to know this? What did Peter's answer reveal about his own conviction? (v. 16)*

5. What did Jesus mean when He said He would build His church "upon this rock"? (v. 18)

_____

_____

6. Why do you think Jesus charged His disciples not to reveal His identity? (v. 20)

_____

_____

7. Why did Jesus call Peter "Satan"? (v. 23)

_____

_____

LESSON AT-A-GLANCE

1. A critical declaration (Matthew 16:13-20)
2. A thoughtless comment (vv. 21-23)

EXPLORING THE MEANING

1. A critical declaration (Matthew 16:13-20)

One day Jesus and His disciples were traveling toward the region of Caesarea Philippi. When they reached the outskirts of this city, Jesus asked His disciples an important question, "Whom do men say that I the Son of man am?" (v. 13)

The 12 men threw out various names they had heard circulated throughout the cities. Some were saying Jesus was John the Baptist (v. 14). Herod had beheaded John the Baptist. When Herod heard of the things Christ did, he feared that Jesus was John returned from the dead (Mark 6:14). Another of the disciples piped in, "Others say Elijah" (Matthew 16:14, NIV). Malachi prophesied that Elijah would return before the coming of the

Messiah (Malachi 4:5). Therefore, some thought He was Elijah. Still others believed Jesus was Jeremiah or one of the prophets (Matthew 16:14). Because of His strong, exhorting message and His compassion toward the people, some believed Jesus was Jeremiah.

The next question Jesus asked is the most far-reaching and personal question that can be asked: "Whom say ye that I am?" (v. 15) The question is critical because what a person believes about Jesus is a prelude to his or her willingness to trust Him for salvation. Faith in Jesus Christ determines whether one receives eternal life or eternal damnation.

The affirmation exploded from Peter's heart to his lips. Without hesitation he responded, "Thou art the Christ, the Son of the living God" (v. 16). Almost three years had passed since Jesus challenged Peter to forsake his fishing profession and join Him in ministry. Peter's bold confession concerning Christ's identity was a measure of how much he had grown under Jesus.

Jesus gave Peter an "A+" for correctly identifying Him as the Christ, the Son of the living God. He called Peter "blessed" (v. 17), because the truth which he spoke did not come from his own reasoning or superior intellect. The heavenly Father had disclosed this information to Peter.

The significance of Peter's confession lies in the fact that if the disciples were going to be Jesus' spokespersons after the resurrection, they would have to be convinced of the Lord's identity.

Then Jesus said, "Thou art Peter, and upon this rock I will build my church" (v. 18). This verse is very controversial. Most Protestants have concluded that the "rock" on which Jesus would build His church was Peter's confession. Most Roman Catholics believe that Peter himself was the rock and this interpretation has led to the tradition of regarding the pope as the titular head of the church. However, "rock" could also refer to Peter's leadership role in evangelism after Jesus' ascension. Peter did open the door of faith to the Jews on the Day of Pentecost (Acts 2:14-41), to the Samaritans (Acts 8:14-25), and also to the Gentiles (Acts 10:34-48).

In Matthew 16:18, we have the first occurrence of the word "church" in the Bible. The Greek word for church is ecclesia and means "called out assembly." The word as Jesus used it here conveys the prediction that all believers (Jew and Gentile) would be joined together in unity. The Apostle Paul described this group as a "body" having many members (1 Corinthians 12). Jesus was doubtlessly referring to the church when He said believers would be the light of the world (5:14).

Jesus assured Peter and the other disciples that even though the forces of evil would be arrayed against the church, they would not prevail. The Lord promised to give Peter the keys of the kingdom of heaven. The keys mentioned in Matthew 16 referred to the exercise of spiritual authority—to open the doors of God's kingdom.

Many scholars believe that the keys represent God's delegated authority to carry out church discipline (Matthew 18:15-18). This is conveyed in the phrase "binding and loosing" (see 16:19), which means forbidding and permitting. The church, as God's representative on earth, exercises full spiritual authority according to His Word. The decisions made on earth would be in keeping with decisions already made by God, indicated by the Greek perfect tense for "shall" used in verse 19.

After making His statements concerning the church, Jesus told the disciples not to tell anyone who He was. Peter's confession of faith opened the door for him to receive blessings from God. He was then given the keys to open the doors of blessings to others. It is only after one opens the door of the heart, through faith, that one comes to know Jesus as the Christ, the Son of the living God.

2. A thoughtless comment (vv. 21-23)

After Jesus received the testimony from Peter that the disciples knew who He was, He went a step further and declared His work. Jesus pointed out that He would suffer and die, that the religious leaders would be His murderers, and Jerusalem (the center of Jewish religious life) would be the place of His death and resurrection (v. 21).

Peter, like the others, was thoroughly confused. They expected the Messiah to overthrow the Roman oppressors, then reign gloriously on earth. He was not supposed to suffer and die. Peter expressed his confusion and concern: "Never, Lord!…This shall never happen to you!" (v. 22, NIV). Peter loved Jesus and sought to protect Him from His grim prophecy. But Jesus immediately responded, "Get thee behind me, Satan: thou art an offence unto me: for thou savourest not the things that be of God, but those that be of men" (v. 23). Even though Peter understood that Jesus was God who had come down to earth to dwell among them, he did not fully understand Christ's mission.

Jesus strongly rebuked Peter because, like Satan, Peter tried to interrupt God's perfect plan to save humanity. Peter "the rock" had become Peter "the stumbling block." The one who moments before had proclaimed divine revelations was now thinking like the devil. When Jesus spoke about His coming trials, Peter forsook God's perspective and evaluated the situation from a human point of view. Peter was like so many of us who have no problem accepting God's will during times of blessing, but see things only from our own perspective during times of testing. Peter never failed to follow Jesus, although he often stumbled. He is an excellent example for all believers to persevere in Christ—even in times of apparent failure.

DISCERNING MY DUTY

1. *Why is it important that people have a correct understanding of who Jesus is? What role can a believer play in helping people to understand Christ's identity?*
2. *If the question, "Who do people say Jesus is?" were put to individuals today, what answers might you get?*
3. *What qualities do you think Jesus saw that led Him to choose Peter to be one of His disciples? Why are these qualities important in building the kingdom of heaven?*
4. *Jesus told His disciples to keep His identity secret. Is there ever a time when we must keep Jesus' identity secret from those who don't know Him?*

DECIDING MY RESPONSE

There seems to be quite a bit of confusion about Jesus' identity. Jesus' life and teachings made it very clear that He is God. The truth is that He left the glories of heaven to become human. As a human, He endured the agonies of the Cross to make possible the restoration of our relationship with the Father. What are some methods the Church and individual believers can use to get this message out to our communities?

Each day this week, praise Jesus Christ for who he is. Look for opportunities to communicate to someone your appreciation for who Jesus is.

LIGHT ON THE HEAVY

Fishers of Men. For centuries, Greek and Roman philosophers used this term to describe the work of the men who seek to "catch" others by teaching and persuasion.

Jesus possibly had seven fishermen in His band of disciples. He knew that these men, because of their profession, would probably be very industrious. A fisherman stayed occupied by mending his nets and preparing for a catch. Fishermen had courage, patience and skill, and were willing to learn from others. A good fisherman had to stay alert. Fishermen had faith that once their nets were thrown into the water, they would bring a bountiful reward. These are the characteristics Jesus wanted in those He chose to be fishers of men.

MORE LIGHT ON THE TEXT

Matthew 16:13 When Jesus came into the coasts of Caesarea Philippi, he asked his disciples, saying, Whom do men say that I the Son of man am?
One of the highest commemorative honors given to a Roman authority was to have places, children, and buildings named after him. Caesarea Philippi was named for two prominent Roman rulers: Caesar Augustus and Philip the Tetrarch. It was here that Jesus, disregarding all of this Roman fanfare, audaciously asks about His own greatness. He wanted to know what the disciples thought of Him. Primarily, Jesus wanted to know if they really knew Him. His reference to Himself as the Son of man (unlike the Gospel of Mark's usage to indicate the humility and suffering) implies exaltation and glory.

14 And they said, Some say that thou art John the Baptist: some, Elias; and others, Jeremias, or one of the prophets.
Jesus is compared to the great prophet Elijah because they performed similar miracles. His being likened to Jeremiah probably

has more to do with Matthew's use of Jeremiah than any correlation between him and Jesus. Jewish history is replete with prophets who told of a Majestic Messiah who was to restore Israel to its rightful political place. Because Jesus' appearance was more lowly than expected, He was believed to have been just a prophet, or even John the Baptist, who was also clothed modestly and unassuming.

15 He saith unto them, But whom say ye that I am?
Although the disciples had seen Jesus perform miracles, cast out demons, and control nature, they still were unsure of His identity. Jesus wanted to know if they knew Him and believed in Him.

16 And Simon Peter answered and said, Thou art the Christ, the Son of the living God.
Simon Peter, whose mother-in-law Jesus healed, made the great confession that Jesus was not just the Son of man, but He was the Son of the living God. Such a confession signifies that Jesus not only has dominion over the earth, but such power comes because of His relationship with the living Creator of the earth. Jesus was the Christ, the Redeemer of Israel, sent by the ever-present, living God of Israel.

17 And Jesus answered and said unto him, "Blessed art thou, Simon Barjona: for flesh and blood hath not revealed it unto thee, but my Father which is in heaven."
Jesus affirmed Simon Peter and his statement and called him "blessed." This word does not merely denote happiness, but is equivalent with having God's kingdom in one's heart and produces satisfaction which comes from God and not the world. For this reason, Jesus told Simon Peter that flesh and blood— a human, earthly body—did not reveal His nature to him; only God could have given such knowledge. Simon, as the son of Jonah

or Bar Jonah, was probably an abbreviated manner of stating that Simon's father was named John.

18 And I say also unto thee, That thou art Peter, and upon this rock I will build my church; and the gates of hell shall not prevail against it.
Simon Peter was no longer Simon Peter; his name now simply meant Peter. He was no longer the infantile disciple wondering who Jesus was, but now securely grounded in the knowledge of this Messiah. Jesus promised to secure the church on Peter's solid confession, not just on Peter. The Greek word for rock, petra, is feminine and does not refer to Peter, but to his statement. Jesus declares that neither Hades, nor Hell, nor any entity will be strong enough to defeat His church.

19 And I will give unto thee the keys of the kingdom of heaven: and whatsoever thou shalt bind on earth shall be bound in heaven: and whatsoever thou shalt loose on earth shall be loosed in heaven.
The issue of binding and loosing deals with the authority the disciples have as followers of Christ and teachers of His Gospel. On earth, the disciples have authority to determine what is applicable to a believer in Christ. In heaven, the binding and loosing refer to their power to pardon sinners in the name of Christ.

20 Then charged he his disciples that they should tell no man that he was Jesus the Christ.
Jesus closed this question and answer period about His identity by telling the disciples that although they knew He was the Messiah, the time had not come for others to know. The disciples, those closest to Jesus, must first be sure of who He was, before others were made aware of Him.

21 From that time forth began Jesus to show unto his disciples, how that he must go unto Jerusalem, and suffer many things of the elders and chief priests and scribes, and be killed, and be raised again the third day.

Since the disciples knew that He was the Messiah, Jesus now told them what the Messiah must do. Jesus the Messiah did not come to overthrow the Roman government and establish a Jewish political kingdom. Instead, Christ came to suffer, die, and be raised. Jesus inferred that Jewish leaders would be involved in his suffering and imminent death. Going to Jerusalem tied in with Matthew's use of the Jewish genealogy in his writing as the Great Jewish King, the Messiah, must always be associated with the city of David. Just as Matthew's Gospel made great efforts to show how Jesus was part of the lineage of David, Jesus' face must always be toward Jerusalem, the city of David.

22 Then Peter took him, and began to rebuke him, saying, Be it far from thee, Lord: this shall not be unto thee.

Peter was still grappling with his image of a conquering Messiah. He was also torn between his own desires for Jesus to remain with him and the other disciples. According to Peter, Jesus should stay, especially now that they knew who He really was. Thus, Jesus the Christ, Peter's Messiah, was not supposed to suffer and die. Peter even stated that the living God should not let this occur.

23 But he turned, and said unto Peter, Get thee behind me, Satan: thou art an offence unto me: for thou savourest not the things that be of God, but those that be of men.

The writer of Matthew shows the dual nature of spirituality and humanity in Peter. First, he was the solid rock who boldly declared that Jesus was the Messiah. Next, he was the stumbling block who could not discern God's will. Therefore, he was referred to as "Satan" because his statement offered the temptation to hold the Messiah and went against the will of God. Peter's fear of what was to come overshadowed his discipleship to the Christ.

Yielding to God's Will
Based on Luke 1:26-38

DEFINING THE ISSUE

Imagine being a young girl in a society that regulates marriage and childbearing with strict laws. Three decades ago, America embraced similar rules. During that time abortions were considered illegal. Premarital and extramarital relations were not the norm. A young woman who became pregnant outside of wedlock was shunned. The man who was responsible was expected to marry the young girl—it was the honorable thing to do. Often parents would send their children away until the child was born. The "illegitimate" children born out of wedlock were affected as well. They were considered mistakes and misfits and frequently had a rough way to go in life. As a result, a woman would never desire to be an unwed mother. It was too difficult.

But think of the ecstatic response of a woman who discovers that she is pregnant because she has aligned her will with God's plan for her life and not because of sin. Such was the case with Mary, the mother of Jesus. She became with child and her pregnancy was holy. Her condition was not the result of promiscuity. It was a result of her willingness to align herself with God's plan for the salvation of the world.

AIM

By the end of this lesson, students will have learned the importance of yielding their lives to God and will respond in wholehearted agreement with and obedience to His will.

SCRIPTURE TEXT

> LUKE 1:26 And in the sixth month the angel Gabriel was sent from God unto a city of Galilee, named Nazareth,
>
> 27 To a virgin espoused to a man whose name was Joseph, of the house of David; and the virgin's name was Mary.
>
> 28 And the angel came in unto her, and said, Hail, thou that art highly favoured, the Lord is with thee: blessed art thou among women.
>
> 29 And when she saw him, she was troubled at his saying, and cast in her mind what manner of salutation this should be.
>
> 30 And the angel said unto her, Fear not, Mary: for thou hast found favour with God.
>
> 31 And, behold, thou shalt conceive in thy womb, and bring forth a son, and shalt call his name JESUS.
>
> 32 He shall be great, and shall be called the Son of the Highest: and the Lord God shall give unto him the throne of his father David.
>
> 33 And he shall reign over the house of Jacob forever; and of his kingdom there shall be no end.

34 Then said Mary unto the angel, How shall this be, seeing I know not a man?

35 And the angel answered and said unto her, The Holy Ghost shall come upon thee, and the power of the Highest shall overshadow thee: therefore also that holy thing which shall be born of thee shall be called the Son of God.

36 And, behold, thy cousin Elisabeth, she hath also conceived a son in her old age: and this is the sixth month with her, who was called barren.

37 For with God nothing shall be impossible.

38 And Mary said, Behold the handmaid of the Lord; be it unto me according to thy word. And the angel departed from her.

BIBLE BACKGROUND

Luke sets his Gospel in the context of the events of the times. John is born in the days of Herod the Great, who ruled from 37-4 B.C. Judea encompasses the entire area of Palestine. The parents of John represent Jewish piety at its best. Zechariah, the father, is a member of one of the 24 divisions of the priesthood. His wife Elizabeth is also of priestly descent. Although they are righteous before God, they had not received the blessing of a child (Luke 1:6-7).

Zechariah belonged to the section of Abia. Every direct descendant of Aaron was automatically a priest. Because there were many priests, they were divided into 24 sections. During the Passover, at Pentecost, and the Feast of Tabernacles all priests served. In addition, each division served twice a year for a period of one week. On this day, the lot fell on Zechariah to burn the incense. He was serving his turn as priest in the temple when the angel appeared to him announcing that he and his wife would have a son who was to be named John. However, Zechariah had doubts that he and his wife would have a son, so for his unbelief he was stricken speechless. Elizabeth conceived and went in hiding and Zechariah was silent, waiting in expectation for the child.

When the child was born Zechariah had a great vision for his son. He thought of him as the prophet and the forerunner who would prepare the way of the Lord. John was born from the priestly family of Aaron and Abijah (1 Chronicles 24:10). He grew up very conscious of the requirements of the law. In the plan of salvation, he was just the right person to serve as the forerunner of the Saviour.

Six months have passed since Gabriel's announcement to Zechariah. Now the Lord sends His messenger on another mission. This time Gabriel goes to a house in Nazareth, not to an aged man but to a young and vibrant maiden. The promised child to Zechariah and Elizabeth was in answer to many prayers; the promised child to Mary was a total and complete surprise. A child born of a virgin—here is something altogether new.

POINTS TO PONDER

1. *In what village was Mary living when the angel visited her? (Luke 1:26)*

    _____

    _____

2. *Name two reasons why Mary was troubled when the angel told her that she would give birth to a son. (vv. 27, 34)*

    _____

    _____

3. *What proof did the angel Gabriel give to Mary to assure her that nothing was impossible for God? (v. 36)*

_____

_____

4. *What did Mary say when the angel Gabriel completed his message? (v. 38)*

_____

_____

LESSON AT-A-GLANCE

1. *Mary receives a visit from the angel Gabriel (Luke 1:26-27)*
2. *Mary receives the announcement of Jesus' birth (vv. 28-33)*
3. *Mary questions Gabriel (vv. 34-37)*
4. *Mary accepts God's will for her life (v. 38)*

EXPLORING THE MEANING

1. Mary receives a visit from the angel Gabriel (Luke 1:26-28)
Nazareth was a small, insignificant village of lower Galilee, with a population of about a hundred people. Nazareth is first mentioned as the home of Mary and Joseph at the time of the annunciation. Although Nathanael asked, "Can anything good come out of Nazareth?" (John 1:46), God sent Gabriel to convey a message to a virgin girl named Mary in this village. Gabriel was one of God's messenger angels. In the Old Testament, he was sent to explain the visions which Daniel saw (Daniel 8:16; 9:21). In the New Testament, Gabriel was sent to announce the birth of John the Baptist (Luke 1:11), and now he was sent by God to the little village of Nazareth to announce the most glorious event of human history.

The angel Gabriel congratulated Mary and told her to rejoice because she had found favor with God. Mary wondered what the angel's message could mean. Why had she found favor with God? Perhaps Mary had found favor with God because of her pureness. She was a virgin waiting to be married. "To be chosen by God so often means at one and the same time a crown of joy and a cross of sorrow. God does not always choose a person for ease and comfort and selfish joy, but for a great task that will take all that head and heart can bring to it. God chooses a person to use that person" (William Barclay, *The Gospel of Luke*, Philadelphia: The Westminster Press, 1975, p. 8).

2. Mary receives the announcement of Jesus' birth (vv. 28-33)
Mary was already "pledged to be married to Joseph" (v. 27). But the angel said to her, "you will conceive in your womb and bring forth a son and you shall call His name Jesus" (v. 31). This was a frightening experience for Mary, because she knew the consequences of not being pure for her marriage. The marriages in antiquity were between families, not individuals, and were parentally arranged. Marriage contracts required extensive negotiation in order to ensure that families of equal status were being joined and that neither took advantage of the other. A couple thus betrothed did not live together, though a formal divorce was required to break the now public agreement. Should the man to whom a girl was betrothed die, in the eyes of the law she was a widow. Once two people were betrothed, there was a bond between them which nothing but death could break. In spite of her pledge to Joseph, God chose Mary to bring forth His Son, the Saviour of the world. She was "the virgin" of prophecy (Isaiah 7:14). The mother of the divine-human person whom Isaiah said was to be "a child" (human) and "Son given" (divine) (John 3:16; 2 Corinthians 9:15). "And He shall reign over Israel forever; His Kingdom shall be forever; His Kingdom shall never end!" (Luke 1:33, LB)

Mary did not find favor with God because she was perfect or unusual, but because she was simply a yielded vessel. The same question may be asked of us today: How can we find favor with God? It is not who we are or what we have that causes us to find favor with God. We find favor with God through humility, a willingness to listen, and obedience to His Word. In other words, we find favor with God by being yielded vessels, willing to do His bidding. God uses simple ordinary people to carry out His will. Mary was a simple, young virgin girl waiting to be married to Joseph and God chose her. She simply yielded to the will of God for her life. When Gabriel spoke to her, she responded by saying, "Let it be according to your word" (v. 38). There are others throughout the New Testament that God chose in spite of themselves.

Saul of Tarsus was a Jew who literally wasted the Christian Church (Acts 8:1). But God chose him, in spite of himself, to minister to the body of Christ. When Saul saw the brightness of God's glory, he fell to the ground. He heard the voice of Jesus asking why he was persecuting Him. Saul was confused because he thought he was doing the will of God. But when he found that he was not doing God's will, he humbled himself and said, "Lord, what wilt thou have me to do?" (Acts 9:6). Saul obeyed and became the Apostle Paul who went about doing the will of God. He had found favor with God.

Martha's sister, Mary, found favor with Jesus by humbly seating herself at His feet. She anointed Jesus' feet with an expensive oil of spikenard and wiped them with her hair (John 12:3). Because of her humility, Mary, the sister of Martha, found favor with Jesus and she is remembered throughout the Christian arena even until today. We don't always know the unique will of God for our lives, but we can find His favor by becoming yielded vessels and keeping ourselves humble and obedient to His Word as Mary did. God has outlined in the Bible all of the commandments and principles that He wants us to follow—line upon line, precept upon precept.

David found favor in God's eyes because he was willing to do God's will. David understood that God could not fail, and that God would never fail him. As a result of David's faith and adoration, God caused him to be blessed and become one of the most revered men in Bible history. The only time David ceased to have God's favor was when he stopped following the will of God. The consequences of sin included losing the throne for a period of time and losing the opportunity to see the temple built.

Mary, the mother of Jesus, found favor with God through her obedience and unconditional faith. Too often, instead of being like Mary, we choose to make the same mistake David made. We fail to enjoy the favor of God because we are blinded by our fleshly desires. During those times, we rationalize that it is okay to disobey the will of God. Mary found favor with God through obedience and submission. We, as believers, can find favor with God the same way.

3. Mary questions Gabriel (vv. 34-37)

Mary asked the angel, "How can this be since I do not know a man? The angel answered and said to her, the Holy Spirit will come upon you and the power of the Highest will overshadow you" (vv. 34-35, NKJV). This means that Christ was placed in the womb of the virgin by a creative act of God, through the power of the Holy Spirit (Matthew 1:18-20). The eternal Son of the Highest miraculously united Himself with human nature in the womb of the virgin (*Unger Bible Handbook*, p. 514). Therefore, the baby that was born to Mary was holy. Deity and humanity united to redeem the human race.

Often, we encounter situations we don't quite understand, and it is necessary for us to ask questions. It can be the loss of a loved one, a job, or finances. It can be overwhelming to hear of some unexpected event that occurs without warning. It does not matter whether it is good news or bad news. The question of how or why will emerge. Mary also asked the question, "How can this be?" After hearing the angel's news, Mary was in a state of confusion and asked the question to determine what was expected of her. It is human nature to want to know the reasons for things. However, we should not doubt God's goodness. Whatever God does is right. God does not chide us for asking questions. But He is disappointed if we conclude that He has forsaken us. By asking questions, we are able to understand what is expected of us. Questions are necessary and the only unanswered question is the question that is not asked.

4. Mary accepts God's will for her life (v. 38)
Mary's reply to the angel was given in the language of faith and humble admiration. She did not ask for a sign to confirm the message. She simply said, "Let it be to me according to your word" (v. 38). Mary of Nazareth surrendered to the will of God. Her response is a model for all believers. She accepted the will of God for her life in humble obedience and without controversy. She glorified God by singing, "My soul magnifies the Lord and my spirit rejoices in God my Savior" (vv. 46-47). Like Mary, we can allow the Word of God to guide our desires and responses.

Joyful acceptance of God's will is a lesson we all can learn as believers in Christ. Many times we say, "Lord have your way in my life," and when God's will is not what we expected, we begin to complain. We sing "Order My Steps" and as soon as He orders them, we groan and question His will. Very often, we struggle with the will of God for our lives because we do not want to obey. There are several stories in the Old Testament of those people who defied the will of God.

Our first parents, Adam and Eve, did not accept the will of God for their lives and disobeyed God (Genesis 3:1-6). Abraham and Sarah were promised a son, and they could not wait for God's will to be fulfilled. Sarah allowed Abraham to be with her bondswoman to bring forth a son (Genesis 16:1ff). Saul, the first king in Israel, also disobeyed God (1 Samuel 15:1ff). These are just to name a few; there are others. It is important for us to realize that God is in control of our lives, and He allows us to be exposed to diverse situations to build our spiritual character. If we would graciously accept God's will, we can say as Mary said, "Let it be according to your word."

DISCERNING MY DUTY

1. *Why do you think God selected a young virgin girl from a village like Nazareth?*
2. *Why did the angel say that "God will give Him the throne of His father David"?*
3. *What is the significance of the Holy Spirit overshadowing Mary for conception?*
4. *If nothing is impossible for God, why do we fret in the face of adversity?*
5. *Why is it hard to yield our will completely to the will of God?*

DECIDING MY RESPONSE

God often acts in ways that baffle human understanding. Does the fact that people cannot explain God and His actions affect their ability to believe in God and obey His will instead of their own?

This week, take a piece of paper and write down your best solution for two situations you are facing. Then pray and ask God to show you His will concerning the two situations you have outlined. Afterward, wait for God to lead you. Because you have written your own solutions down, you might find it easier to know when the Lord is directing you and when you are directing yourself.

LIGHT ON THE HEAVY

The Angel Gabriel. Gabriel is mentioned four times in Scripture. His first appearance is as a man in a vision (Daniel 8:16). He is called "the man Gabriel" and explained to Daniel the vision of the 70 weeks (9:21). In the New Testament, he is mentioned in the Gospel narratives in connection with the story of the birth of Jesus and John the Baptist (Luke 1:11-20). In Luke 1:26-38, he announces the birth of a Son to Mary. Gabriel stands in the presence of God (1:19) and can therefore provide reassurance to mortals: "Do not be afraid, for your prayer is heard (v. 13); "Do not be afraid, Mary for you have found favor with God" (v. 30) (*The Interpreter's Dictionary*, p. 333).

Born a Saviour
Based on Luke 2:4-20

DEFINING THE ISSUE

For two centuries, African Americans were slaves with seemingly no hope for deliverance. As they toiled in wretched conditions, they sang songs and prayed prayers, hoping for relief. God heard their cries, and He allowed someone to rise among them. Her name was Harriet Tubman and she was known as the "Moses" of her people.

Tubman was born in slavery and experienced many hardships. Unlike some who had accepted their lot, she longed for freedom. And God did indeed allow her to escape the bonds of slavery. She enjoyed her freedom, but she couldn't forget her brothers and sisters who were still in bondage. She returned to the South many times and led her people to freedom, just as Moses had done in Egypt for his people.

The slaves were clever. They included coded escape signals in their songs. After dark, "Steal Away" was the song used to signal slaves to move to a meeting place from which they would escape to the North by the Underground Railroad. Harriet Tubman helped more than 300 slaves escape to freedom this way. And though she only delivered a relatively few from the bonds of slavery, her heroic deeds focused attention on the need for emancipation.

Moses, Harriet Tubman, Martin Luther King, Jr., and others were powerful leaders who were led by God. Each came to lead a particular people at a particular time. However, Jesus came for ALL people and His great work has and will be felt throughout all eternity. Our lesson today calls our attention to the birth of Jesus, a Saviour for the world.

AIM

By the end of the lesson, students will be able to explain the importance of Christ's humble birth, give reports of praise for the good things God is doing in their lives and the lives of others, and participate this week in a class sharing project in appreciation for what Christ means to them.

SCRIPTURE TEXT

> LUKE 2:4 And Joseph also went up from Galilee, out of the city of Nazareth, into Judaea, unto the city of David, which is called Bethlehem; (because he was of the house and lineage of David:)
>
> 5 To be taxed with Mary his espoused wife, being great with child.
>
> 6 And so it was, that, while they were there, the days were accomplished that she should be delivered.
>
> 7 And she brought forth her firstborn son, and wrapped him in swaddling clothes, and laid him in a manger; because there was no room for them in the inn.
>
> 8 And there were in the same country shepherds abiding in the field, keeping watch over their flock by night.

9 And, lo, the angel of the Lord came upon them, and the glory of the Lord shone round about them: and they were sore afraid.

10 And the angel said unto them, Fear not: for, behold, I bring you good tidings of great joy, which shall be to all people.

11 For unto you is born this day in the city of David a Saviour, which is Christ the Lord.

12 And this shall be a sign unto you; Ye shall find the babe wrapped in swaddling clothes, lying in a manger.

13 And suddenly there was with the angel a multitude of the heavenly host praising God, and saying,

14 Glory to God in the highest, and on earth peace, good will toward men.

15 And it came to pass, as the angels were gone away from them into heaven, the shepherds said one to another, Let us now go even unto Bethlehem, and see this thing which is come to pass, which the Lord hath made known unto us.

16 And they came with haste, and found Mary, and Joseph, and the babe lying in a manger.

17 And when they had seen it, they made known abroad the saying which was told them concerning this child.

18 And all they that heard it wondered at those things which were told them by the shepherds.

19 But Mary kept all these things, and pondered them in her heart.

20 And the shepherds returned, glorifying and praising God for all the things that they had heard and seen, as it was told unto them.

BIBLE BACKGROUND

The Jerome Biblical Commentary aptly singles out Luke 2:4-21 as the epitome of Lucan artistry. Luke ties the birth of Jesus in Bethlehem to the figures of Herod the Great, Caesar Augustus, and Quirinius under whom the census took place. It is clear that Luke wrote mainly for Gentiles. Theophilus is Gentile, as is Luke himself, and there is nothing in the Gospel that a Gentile could not understand.

Luke painstakingly recreates the social history for the reader. He tries to show us what was taking place at the time of the birth of Jesus in both the Hebrew and Gentile communities and the Roman Empire. In verses 8-14, we have the angels' poignant and exhilarating pronouncement of the divine birth. That the pronouncement came to shepherds is significant because it points to King David's origin as a shepherd. Also, "the shepherds were despised by the orthodox good people of the day. Shepherds were quite unable to keep the details of the ceremonial law; they could not observe all the meticulous hand-washings and rules and regulations. Their flocks made far too constant demands on them; and so the orthodox looked down on them as a very common people" (William Barclay, *The Gospel of Luke*, Philadelphia: The Westminster Press, 1975, p. 22).

Moreover, the shepherds' humble lifestyle offers encouragement to those who lack religious status. The shepherds' lifestyle is also typical of the life Jesus would lead during His ministry on earth. Jesus would be unorthodox, not too concerned about hand-washing, and would circulate with the common people. His life would mirror the lives of the shepherds.

The shepherds were overtaken with excitement when the announcement was made to them by the angel. They immediately went to Bethlehem to see that the birth of Jesus was true. They found the Babe just as the angel announced.

POINTS TO PONDER

1. *Why did Joseph go to Bethlehem? (Luke 2:4)*

2. *Describe the heavenly visitation to the shepherds who were watching their flocks. (v. 9)*

3. *What type of news did the angels have for the shepherds? (v. 10)*

4. *What sign did the angels give the shepherds to identify the Babe? (v. 12)*

5. *How did Mary react to Jesus' birth? (v. 19)*

6. *What did the shepherds do after they left Mary and the Babe? (v. 20)*

LESSON AT-A-GLANCE

1. *The Christ is born (Luke 2:4-7)*
2. *The Christ's birth is celebrated by angels (vv. 8-14)*
3. *The Christ is visited by shepherds (vv. 15-19)*
4. *The Christ's birth brings glory to God (v. 20)*

EXPLORING THE MEANING

1. The Christ is born (Luke 2:4-7)

It was prophesied (Isaiah 9:6-7) that a child would be born to implement a righteous government that would be based on judgment and justice. Through God's divine providence working through Caesar Augustus, an imperial enrollment decree went out for all to be counted. Joseph and Mary had to go Bethlehem to register because Joseph was from the lineage of David. "The journey from Nazareth to Bethlehem was 80 miles in length. The accommodations for travelers were in any case most primitive.... The town was crowded and there was no room for Joseph and Mary" (William Barclay, *The Gospel of Luke*, Philadelphia: The Westminster Press, 1975, p. 22). While there, the time came for Mary to give birth to the Child that would be the Saviour of the world. Finding no room in the inn, and with Mary's delivery time being near, they were compelled to go to a stable. After Mary gave birth to Jesus, she wrapped Him in swaddling clothes and laid Him in a manger. In the meantime, the angel of the Lord made the announcement to some shepherds to go to the city of David and see "a Saviour, which is Christ the Lord" (Luke 2:11).

Bethlehem was crowded and everything was in an upheaval because of the registration. But Jesus was coming to town and there was no room to receive Him. This is so like our lives. Often, we are so taken up with our personal agendas that we neglect to recognize the presence of Jesus. We look for Him in the wrong places and He is not there. He is most at home with humble people, those who take time to let Him into their daily activities. He is with the people who have room for Him in their hearts. He is with the person who hears the voice of the Lord through the Word that points to Jesus. The shepherds were eager to listen to the voice of the angels directing them to where they would find Jesus. Humble people listen to those who are directing them to where they can find Jesus. He is waiting for us with open arms.

2. The Christ's birth is celebrated by angels (vv. 8-14)

Angels, focused on doing the total will of God and not confined to time and space, were used to announce the birth of Jesus. As they made the announcement, they celebrated by worshiping and glorifying God. To worship and praise God is part of their character. They joined with the heavenly host in saying: "Glory to God in the highest, and on earth peace, to men on whom his favor rests" (Luke 2:14, NIV). When the angels returned to heaven, the shepherds went immediately to Bethlehem to visit Jesus. How wonderful it would be if today we celebrated the birth of Jesus rather than human substitutes.

3. The Christ is visited by shepherds (vv. 15-19)

The fact that the angelic announcement came to shepherds is significant. A shepherd cares for flocks of sheep. He leads the sheep to pasture, to water and, at night, to the fold for safety. The shepherd is responsible for protecting the flock from wild animals. The shepherd and sheep motif typifies the role of Jesus as Saviour. He was born to be the Messiah, to lead the "flock," God's people, and to serve the flock as the Lamb of God. Jesus referred to Himself as the "good shepherd" (John 10:11).

Unlike many of us today who would probably question any miracle we might be privileged to witness, the shepherds humbly accepted the angel's message and acted immediately. They went to Bethlehem to see the Baby Jesus. The fact that the shepherds found Jesus lying in a manger was their confirmation that Jesus was the expected Messiah who was prophesied about by the Prophet Isaiah: "For unto us a child is born, unto us a son is given; and the government shall be upon his shoulder" (Isaiah 9:6a).

The shepherds relayed the angelic message concerning Jesus' birth (Luke 2:17). Those who heard their message were utterly amazed at the events unfolding before their eyes. Mary kept the message in her heart (vv. 18-19). Indeed, Mary pondered many things in her heart (vv. 17-19). She constantly received and watched as prophecies were fulfilled through her Son (see v. 51).

We can learn much from Mary. We can learn how to: (a) meditate and ponder the message God gives us through His word; (b) be obedient to the Word of God; (c) celebrate the will of God for our lives; and (d) give God praise as Mary did. She said, "My soul magnifies the Lord, and my spirit has rejoiced in God my Saviour" (Luke 1:46-47, NKJV). Yes, Mary celebrated the will of God for her life. So can we.

4. The Christ's birth brings glory to God (v. 20)

Christ's birth brings glory to God because He is the fulfillment of God's promise. Jesus is the One John said would come after him, whose sandal strap John would not feel worthy to untie (Luke 3:16). Christ brings glory to God because He is the Saviour of the world. God gives His Son so that whoever believes in Him can be saved (John 3:16b).

After visiting Mary and Joseph and finding the Baby Jesus wrapped in swaddling clothes, "the shepherds returned, glorifying and praising God for all the things that they had heard and seen, as it was told unto them" (Luke 2:20).

DISCERNING MY DUTY

1. *What was significant about the shepherds?*
2. *Why was Jesus born in a stable?*
3. *Why was there suddenly a host of angels singing praises to God at Jesus' birth? How do we celebrate the incarnation (God becoming flesh) of Christ? How do we show appreciation for other blessings God gives?*
4. *Why do you think Mary pondered everything in her heart?*
5. *Did the shepherds doubt what the angels said?*

DECIDING MY RESPONSE

In today's society, we are drawn to tragedy and bad news. We cause traffic jams by "gaping" at accidents. We buy magazines about scandals. And we clog our conversations with negative things we've heard concerning other people.

1. *In your opinion, what is it about negative news that fascinates us?*
2. *List three or four ways that the church can influence newspapers, radio, and television to increase coverage of positive news.*

Look ahead to the opportunities that you may have to talk with people in the coming week. Make a point each day to tell someone about some of the wonderful things that have happened to you or other people that you know. Also, encourage others to share their good news. Greet people with the question, "What's the good news?" At the end of the week, note any changes in your perspective on life which result from your new conversations.

LIGHT ON THE HEAVY

Praise. To praise is to extol and give thanks. Praising God is much more important than merely talking about God. God is our object of praise (Deuteronomy 10:21), and thereby the superiority and uniqueness of God's divine person and activity are set forth.

Praise attempts to describe God, but it can only offer a limited description. There are eight instances in the New Testament that refer to the joyful praise of God through the hymns or prayers of individuals (Luke 2:20; Acts 3:8-9), a group (Luke 19:37), the community (Acts 2:47; Revelation 19:5), angels (Luke 2:13), or within a religious setting (Matthew 21:16; Luke 18:43). We honor God when we praise Him. Isn't that beautiful?

The Book of Psalms is filled with praise and adoration for God. Chapters 113-118 are called the "Hallel" (hallel is the root word for hallelujah which means praise). Psalms 120-136 are often called the "Great Hallel." Hallelujah is one of the highest praises we can give to the Lord. (*The New Compact Bible Dictionary*, p. 471).

MORE LIGHT ON THE TEXT

Luke 2:4 And Joseph also went up from Galilee, out of the city of Nazareth, into Judaea, unto the city of David, which is called Bethlehem; (because he was of the house and lineage of David:)
Joseph went to Bethlehem, the city of David, because he was a descendant of David. Bethlehem was the Judean village of David's origin. The Messiah must be born in the city of David. Luke, therefore, emphasized this fact for the purpose of storytelling and establishing Jesus' messianic credentials. Thus, Mary and Joseph came to Bethlehem before the Baby was born.

5 To be taxed with Mary his espoused wife, being great with child.
Luke did not refer to Mary as Joseph's wife although technically Jewish law stated that he could have, since they were engaged. Unlike Matthew, he was primarily silent about Joseph's reactions to Mary's pregnancy.

6 And so it was, that, while they were there, the days were accomplished that she should be delivered.
To validate His messianic identity, Jesus was born in Bethlehem. The timing of the census and the pregnancy set the context for Luke's story.

7 And she brought forth her firstborn son, and wrapped him in swaddling clothes, and laid him in a manger; because there was no room for them in the inn.
A firstborn son was considered a special blessing in Jewish families and received a privileged role. Strips or bands of cloth were wrapped around a newborn to keep the limbs straight by means of restraint. One would think that Joseph would stay with family members since he was from Bethlehem, but Luke established the meekness of the birth of the Messiah by stating that not a main room in a home nor even an attached room for guests was available for the Messiah. The Greek word for inn, *kataluma*, implies lodging and could refer to either place.

8 And there were in the same country shepherds abiding in the field, keeping watch over their flock by night.
Luke continued to describe the setting into which the "Anointed One" was born. His place of birth was merely a feeding area for animals. Luke connected the city of David with the shepherds, since David was also a shepherd before he was anointed king.

9 And, lo, the angel of the Lord came upon them, and the glory of the Lord shone round about them: and they were sore afraid.
Luke included this third appearance by an angel (See Luke 1:5- 23, 26-38). This appearance, however, was not to a parent, but to all people. Also, the shepherds did not protest what the angel told them. The glory or *doxa* indicates splendor and the presence of light in the midst of darkness. It was this light that naturally frightened the shepherds.

10 And the angel said unto them, Fear not: for, behold, I bring you good tidings of great joy, which shall be to all people.
Recognizing the shepherds' fear, the angel tried to assuage them. The angel brought the news of the visitation of God among His people in an authoritative yet calming fashion. The angel brought news that would bring joy or (Greek) *chara*, that is messianic exaltation and peace.

11 For unto you is born this day in the city of David a Savior, which is Christ the Lord.
The city of David is mentioned again to add credibility to Jesus' role as the Messiah. He was not only the Messiah, but the Saviour. This referred to His role as both messianic king and heir to David's throne. He is Saviour because He alone can grant forgiveness of sin.

12 And this shall be a sign unto you; Ye shall find the babe wrapped in swaddling clothes, lying in a manger.
The sign was not the child's circumstances, but the fact that what the angel had described to the shepherds was true. It was the fulfilling of a prophecy about Jesus (Isaiah 7:14).

13 And suddenly there was with the angel a multitude of the heavenly host praising God, and saying
"Heavenly host" implies a large, gathered number. It was the armies of heaven whose testimony revealed the divine meaning of this birth.

14 Glory to God in the highest, and on earth peace, good will toward men.
The Greek word *eudokia* can be read as good will or favor. Thus, the verse can read peace among people of good will. Where the peace of God is present, there is good will and favor. The phrasing is altered in Luke 19:38 where peace was declared in heaven and glory in the highest heaven.

15 And it came to pass, as the angels were gone away from them into heaven, the shepherds said one to another, Let us now go even unto Bethlehem, and see this thing which is come to pass, which the Lord hath made known unto us.
After overcoming their fear, the shepherds responded by going to Bethlehem in order to verify the angels' message. Hearing the heavenly message caused them to respond in action.

16 And they came with haste, and found Mary, and Joseph, and the babe lying in a manger.
"With haste" implies that they hurried and went with much anticipation.

17 And when they had seen it, they made known abroad the saying which was told them concerning this child.
The shepherds told those who were in the company of Mary and Joseph what the angel and heavenly host told them about the Baby Jesus and His identity. This verse does not imply that the shepherds were telling the townspeople as yet, but they wanted Mary and Joseph to know the message they had received and from whom it came.

Coping With Doubts and Fears
Based on Luke 24:36-53

DEFINING THE ISSUE

It has been reported by researchers that more than 85 percent of the things we fear never happen. Why, then, do we harbor so many fears and doubts?

In this lesson, we will study how Jesus dealt with the doubts of His disciples after His resurrection. Jesus' example provides a pattern for dealing with our own doubts and fears.

AIM

By the end of the lesson, students will discover how Jesus dealt with the doubts and fears of His disciples, become convinced that trusting in Jesus can lead to less worry in their lives, and determine to cast their cares upon Jesus, trusting Him to give them peace in the midst of the storms of life.

SCRIPTURE TEXT

> LUKE 24:36 And as they thus spake, Jesus himself stood in the midst of them, and saith unto them, Peace be unto you.

37 But they were terrified and affrighted, and supposed that they had seen a spirit.

38 And he said unto them, Why are ye troubled? and why do thoughts arise in your hearts?

39 Behold my hands and my feet, that it is I myself: handle me, and see; for a spirit hath not flesh and bones, as ye see me have.

40 And when he had thus spoken, he showed them his hands and his feet.

41 And while they yet believed not for joy, and wondered, he said unto them, Have ye here any meat?

42 And they gave him a piece of a broiled fish, and of an honeycomb.

43 And he took it, and did eat before them.

44 And he said unto them, These are the words which I spake unto you, while I was yet with you, that all things must be fulfilled, which were written in the law of Moses, and in the prophets, and in the psalms, concerning me.

45 Then opened he their understanding, that they might understand the scriptures,

46 And said unto them, Thus it is written, and thus it behooved Christ to suffer, and to rise from the dead the third day:

47 And that repentance and remission of sins should be preached in his name among all nations, beginning at Jerusalem.

48 And ye are witnesses of these things.

49 And, behold, I send the promise of my Father upon you: but tarry ye in the city of Jerusalem, until ye be endued with power from on high.

50 And he led them out as far as to Bethany, and he lifted up his hands, and blessed them.

51 And it came to pass, while he blessed them, he was parted from them, and carried up into heaven.

52 And they worshiped him, and returned to Jerusalem with great joy:

53 And were continually in the temple, praising and blessing God. Amen.

BIBLE BACKGROUND

Jesus reacted to the fears of His disciples by asking two questions, "Why are ye troubled? And why do thoughts arise in your hearts?"

First, the disciples were troubled because they did not fully realize the character and power of Jesus Christ. Second, the disciples apparently did not remember the promise of God to raise Jesus from the dead after three days. Third, the disciples did not understand the Scriptures. And fourth, they had not accepted the evidence before them, the risen Christ.

From the Gospel account, it is clear that no person or thing, except the presence of Jesus Himself, could convince His confused disciples that He had indeed arisen. The words of the angels, the testimony of the women, the reports of Peter and the men of Emmaus were not sufficient to reassure the rest of the disciples that Christ was alive. These testimonies caused hope to flare up now and then, but all doubts were banished only by Jesus Himself.

POINTS TO PONDER

1. *What did Jesus ask the disciples to do in order to convince them that He was not a spirit? (vv. 39-40, 43)*

2. *What did Jesus say to the disciples which reminded them that His death and resurrection were foretold in the Jewish Scriptures? (v. 44)*

3. *What did Jesus do that enabled the disciples to understand the Scriptures? (v. 45)*

4. *The message Christ instructed the apostles to preach was twofold. What are the two parts of the message? (vv. 46-47)*

5. *To whom were the disciples to preach the Gospel first? Second? (v. 47)*

6. *Why were the disciples chosen to preach the Gospel? (v. 48)*

7. *Why were the disciples to tarry in Jerusalem (v. 49)*

8. *What did Jesus do when He and the disciples reached Bethany? (v. 50)*

_____

_____

9. *What did the disciples do after Jesus was carried up into heaven? (vv. 51-52)*

_____

_____

LESSON AT-A-GLANCE

1. *Christ presented proof (Luke 24:36-43)*
2. *Christ reviewed the promises (v. 44)*
3. *Christ discussed the meaning of the Promise (v. 45)*
4. *Christ explained the plan (vv. 46-47)*
5. *Christ promised to be supportive (v. 48)*
6. *Christ trusted His disciples (vv. 50-53)*

EXPLORING THE MEANING

1. Christ presented proof (Luke 24:36-43)

While the disciples and other followers of Jesus were talking about the events of the week behind closed doors, and while the struggle between hope and despair was still raging in many an ear, the Saviour suddenly stood amongst them. All the doors were shut (John 20:19). Jesus appeared by supernatural power; He was already glorified. As the risen Christ, He was able to appear and disappear at will. His resurrected body was no longer bound by the limitations of His earthly body.

Because Christ's appearance was unexpected, the disciples were initially terrified. Jesus calmed the fears and erased the doubts of

His disciples by presenting Himself as evidence that He was alive. To assure them that they had not seen a "spirit," first Jesus established the premise that "a spirit had not flesh and bones" (Luke 24:39). To do this, Jesus appealed to the disciples' most powerful senses—the senses of sight and touch.

First, Jesus showed the disciples His nail-pierced hands and feet. Bible scholars state that Jesus retained these markings in His glorified body so that the disciples could identify Him as the man they had seen crucified. Second, Jesus invited the disciples to touch Him. Why did Jesus insist that His disciples examine Him? Jesus realized that to preach His resurrection, the disciples must be convinced beyond a reasonable doubt that He had truly been resurrected. Touching was one method Jesus used to help convince the disciples that He was alive.

The third thing Jesus did to convince the disciples that He was alive was to eat and drink with them. Later, Peter presents this action as indisputable evidence that Jesus is alive—"We did eat and drink with Him after He rose from the dead" (Acts 10:41).

Christ dealt with His disciples' doubts by presenting proof that the Person they were looking at was really the Person they had seen crucified.

2. Christ reviewed the promises (v. 44)

One reason for doubt is insufficient information. Jesus explained to His disciples that every prophecy about Him in the Old Testament had to be fulfilled. Jesus reminded His disciples that He had already told them concerning these prophecies, "while I was yet with you."

Christ continued to refresh the memories of the disciples by mentioning the parts of the Old Testament which contained prophecies concerning Himself: the Law of Moses, the Prophets, and the Psalms. These are the three main divisions of the Jewish canon of Scriptures in which God revealed His will concerning Christ and His kingdom.

Matthew Henry states, "We should better understand what Christ does, if we did but better remember what He hath said." To banish the doubts of His disciples, Christ rehearsed the facts concerning His purpose on earth as revealed in the Scriptures.

3. Christ discussed the meaning of the promise (v. 45)

Early in the week, Jesus had explained the meaning of the Old Testament Scriptures to the men of Emmaus (v. 27). Now by a supernatural work, He enabled them to understand the true intent and meaning of the Old Testament prophecies of Christ. In His conversation with the two disciples on Emmaus road, "He took the veil from off the text, by opening the Scriptures; here He took the veil from off the heart, by opening the mind" (Matthew Henry).

To eliminate the doubts of His disciples, Christ discussed the meaning of the Scriptures concerning Himself.

4. Christ explained the plan (vv. 46-47)

Jesus dispelled doubt in the minds of His disciples concerning whether or not they could continue the work by explaining the plan they would use to spread the salvation message.

   A. What message were the disciples instructed to preach? First, they must preach that Christ suffered and rose from the dead on the third day (v. 46). These two facts—Christ's suffering and resurrection—became the theme of all apostolic preaching and teaching (1 Corinthians 15:3). And second, "repentance and remission of sins" was to be preached in Christ's name and by His authority (v. 47). These were the doctrines preached by the apostles at Pentecost (Acts 2:38).

B. To whom were the disciples to preach? The disciples must preach the Gospel "among all nations, beginning at Jerusalem" (v. 47). The preaching of the Gospel was to take place first in Jerusalem among the Jewish people, but the message of salvation must also be made known to all nations of the world. In the second part of Isaiah, it is clearly prophesied that the ultimate purpose of the divine revelation was that the glad tidings of salvation must be brought to all people (Isaiah 42:6; 45:22). To eliminate the disciples' apprehension about continuing the work after He returned to heaven, Christ explained in detail the plan He wanted the disciples to carry out.

5. Christ promised to be supportive (v. 48)

The tremendous responsibility of preaching the Gospel rests on those who witnessed Christ's death and resurrection. In their own strength the disciples knew that they would never be able to do what Christ had asked them to do. However, Jesus assured His disciples that he would provide emotional and spiritual support. Christ gave His disciples emotional support by promising to be with them always, "even unto the end of the world" (Matthew 28:20). By promising to send the Holy Spirit, Christ assured His disciples of spiritual support.

Christ promised the disciples that His Father would send the Holy Spirit to dwell in His Church and in them individually. The Holy Spirit would equip them with His divine strength so that they could perform the great task to which they had been called as witnesses.

To eliminate all doubts and fears, Christ promised His disciples emotional and spiritual support.

6. Christ trusted His disciples (vv. 50-53)

Finally, Jesus expressed trust in His disciples by physically leaving them alone. In everything, Christ obeyed and honored His Father. Now His work had been completed. He came from heaven, finished His work on earth, and He returned to heaven (v. 51).

Often doubts arise in the lives of believers when they do not trust the person for whom they are waiting, nor understand why they are waiting. Contrast the difference between the actions of the disciples as they waited for Jesus after His crucifixion and as they waited for the Holy Spirit after Christ's ascension. The length of time the disciples waited for the Holy Spirit (40 days) was much longer than the time they had waited for Jesus' appearance after His resurrection. But there is no record that the disciples doubted nor wavered in their faith as they waited for the Holy Spirit in Jerusalem.

Who else can banish all fear from our hearts and give us the inward rest and peace which enables us to act as living witnesses of our living Redeemer?

DISCERNING MY DUTY

Why was it important that:

1. *Christ present Himself to His disciples before leaving them?*
2. *Christ review the promises concerning His death and resurrection?*
3. *Christ discuss the meaning of the Scriptures concerning Himself?*
4. *Christ explain His plan to spread the Gospel throughout the world to his disciples?*
5. *Christ promise to support the disciples emotionally and spiritually?*
6. *Christ trust His disciples to carry on His work?*

DECIDING MY RESPONSE

Whenever you are tempted to doubt God's power to perform His will in and through you, remember to:

1. *Read your Bible to discover proof that God has already performed a similar action for someone else.*
2. *Read your Bible to discover and/or review His promises concerning your problem.*
3. *Pray that God will "open your understanding" of the Scriptures concerning your problem.*
4. *Read your Bible to receive assurance that Jesus Christ will support you during your crisis; pray to sense His support during your crisis.*
5. *Finally, when you are victorious, share your experience with someone.*

LIGHT ON THE HEAVY

Bethany. A village located at the Mount of Olives. Its modern name is *El-Azariyeh* or *Lazarich*. The town is about two miles east of Jerusalem near the road from Jericho to the city. (Youngs Analytical Concordance, Grand Rapids, MI, Eardman Publishing 1955, p. 91).

MORE LIGHT ON THE TEXT

Luke 24:36 And as they thus spake, Jesus himself stood in the midst of them, and saith unto them, Peace be unto you.
In Luke's narrative, this Scripture describes the third appearance of the risen Christ (24:13-31; 24:34). One could say that these appearances correlate with the three days Christ was dead. The greeting of "Peace" resonates in Luke because Jesus is portrayed

as the prophet whose visitation of the people is a proclamation of peace. Peace or (Greek) *eirene* in this verse denotes "good wishes."

This greeting was also common among the Jews and in this verse is a sign of the kingdom.

37 But they were terrified and affrighted, and supposed that they had seen a spirit.
Luke uses the Greek word *phantasma* (not *pneuma* meaning spirit) to describe what the disciples thought they were seeing. They thought Jesus was an apparition or phantom of some sort.

38 And he said unto them, Why are you troubled? and why do thoughts arise in your hearts?
At Jesus' birth, as documented in the Gospel of Luke, the shepherds were frightened by the angels. The author continues to describe the human response of fear by showing how these men were also frightened after Jesus' resurrection.

39 Behold my hands and my feet, that it is I myself: handle me, and see; for a spirit hath not flesh and bones, as ye see me have.
The feet and bones imagery serve to demonstrate the physical reality of Jesus. He was a real being. This imagery also is used to show Jesus' relationship with humanity. The Greek word, *pselaphao*, or touch, means to examine closely.

40 And when he had thus spoken, he shewed them his hands and his feet. 41 And while they yet believed not for joy, and wondered, he said unto them. Have ye here any meat?
The men had joy (*chara*—gladness or rejoicing) and yet, were still confused. Luke establishes that the emotional response of the disciples was so powerful that they were too overwhelmed to believe.

It is also possible that they were still reflecting on the fact that they had witnessed the horrible death of Jesus.

42 And they gave him a piece of broiled fish. 43 And he took it, and did eat before them.
Eating the broiled fish emphasized the reality of the resurrection. Jesus ate in order to confirm His physical nature. Fish and bread were the same foods Jesus had used to feed the multitudes.

44 And he said unto them, These are the words which I spake unto you, while I was yet with you, that all things must be fulfilled, which were written in the law of Moses, and in the prophets, and in the psalms, concerning me.
This section raises the issue of prophecy and fulfillment in order to show Jesus' death and resurrection as a part of God's scriptural plan. Jesus began to interpret Israel's Scriptures to show that the Messiah's suffering was necessary to fulfill God's plan of salvation.

45 Then opened he their understanding, that they might understand the scriptures,
Jesus wanted to eliminate the disciples' confusion and disbelief by using Scriptures to confirm and clarify all that happened to Him.

46 And said unto them, Thus it is written, and thus it behooved Christ to suffer, and to rise from the dead the third day:
By using the Scriptures, Jesus reminded the disciples of the prophecy about Him and showed how it reached fulfillment.

47 And that repentance and remission of sins should be preached in his name among all nations, beginning at Jerusalem.
Repentance and forgiveness of sins is the substance of the mission as later stressed in Acts 2:38. Now that prophecy had been fulfilled, the disciples must minister to all. "Beginning from Jerusalem"

emphasized the need to proclaim the Gospel to the Jews and the Gentiles. It was a statement of inclusion, not sequential priority.

48 And ye are witnesses of these things.
The disciples were witnesses of Jesus because they had been taught by Him, worked with Him, and had their minds opened by Him to understand Scripture. Therefore, they could share with others what Jesus had shared with them. The word "witness" or in the Greek, *martus*, refers to one who has information or knowledge of something or one who can give light or confirm something. *Martus* also denotes those who have suffered death as a consequence of confessing Christ. Thus, Jesus alluded to the deaths of His disciples.

49 And, behold, I send the promise of my Father upon you: but tarry ye in the city of Jerusalem, until ye be endued with power from on high.
Jesus promised the disciples that they would receive the Holy Spirit, power from on high. This Spirit had power for their mission of proclamation.

50 And he led them out as far as to Bethany, and he lifted up his hands, and blessed them.
Bethany was approximately two miles from Jerusalem on the lower slope of the Mount of Olives. Here Jesus blessed them in a priestly manner. It is similar to Moses lifting his hands to give the Israelites victory and to Aaron raising his hands and blessing the people.

51 And it came to pass, while he blessed them, he was parted from them, and carried up into heaven.
Jesus' ascension was not only His departure from earth, but His exaltation to the right hand of God, where He is enthroned as

ruling Messiah. Thus, Luke began and ended the Gospel with Jesus' Messianic fulfillment.

52 And they worshipped him, and returned to Jerusalem with great joy:
The Greek word for worship, *proskyneo*, means that the disciples fell prostrate on their faces, in a form of homage, reverence, and deep respect for their superior authority, Christ. This joy or *chara* signifies a state of messianic exaltation and peace.

53 And were continually in the temple, praising and blessing God. Amen.
No longer confused, the disciples expressed their joy by constantly blessing God in the temple. Just as action in this Gospel began in the temple with joy as a key component, so did the Gospel end in the temple and with joy.

Do As I Have Done
Based on John 13:1-8, 12-17, 34-35

DEFINING THE ISSUE

Brian was a young man who felt unloved. He was really not that different from anyone, but he felt he was. His parents had a truce in their house—they each did what they wanted and stayed out of each other's way. Brian just watched from the middle, and though he was given (or able to get) almost everything he wanted, his parents took no personal interest in him. He got married when he was only 19, trying to find "love," but that only made things worse. He wasn't ready for marriage—neither was his wife—so they fought, had a baby, and separated.

Right now, Brian is still looking for love. Love from others could give him assurance that he is somebody, help him get himself together, and perhaps even help him make something out of his mistakes.

Could Brian find love in your church? Can the elderly, the college student, the divorced woman, the "different" ones, find love in your church?

AIM

By the end of the lesson, students should be able to tell the story of Jesus washing His disciples' feet, express something of its spiritual significance, and decide to perform an act of loving service this week.

SCRIPTURE TEXT

JOHN 13:1 Now before the feast of the passover, when Jesus knew that his hour was come that he should depart out of this world unto the Father, having loved his own which were in the world, he loved them unto the end.

2 And supper being ended, the devil having now put into the heart of Judas Iscariot, Simon's son, to betray him;

3 Jesus knowing that the Father had given all things into his hands, and that he was come from God, and went to God;

4 He riseth from supper, and laid aside his garments; and took a towel, and girded himself.

5 After that he poureth water into a basin, and began to wash the disciples' feet, and to wipe them with the towel wherewith he was girded.

6 Then cometh he to Simon Peter: and Peter saith unto him, Lord, dost thou wash my feet?

7 Jesus answered and said unto him, What I do thou knowest not now; but thou shalt know hereafter.

8 Peter saith unto him, Thou shalt never wash my feet. Jesus answered him, If I wash thee not, thou hast no part with me.

12 So after he had washed their feet, and had taken his garments, and was set down again, he said unto them, Know ye what I have done to you?

13 Ye call me Master and Lord: and ye say well; for so I am.

14 If I then, your Lord and Master, have washed your feet; ye also ought to wash one another's feet.

15 For I have given you an example, that ye should do as I have done to you.

16 Verily, verily, I say unto you, The servant is not greater than his lord; neither he that is sent greater than he that sent him.

17 If ye know these things, happy are ye if ye do them.

34 A new commandment I give unto you, That ye love one another; as I have loved you, that ye also love one another.

35 By this shall all men know that ye are my disciples, if you have love one to another.

BIBLE BACKGROUND

By the time the events recorded in the 13th chapter of John's Gospel occur, Jesus' public ministry has ended and He is alone with the 12 disciples. Of the Gospel writers, only John provides this intimate view of Jesus' private teaching and prayer (Chapters 13-17). The 13th chapter records the events of the night before the Crucifixion—the eating of the Passover and the institution of the Lord's Supper (compare Matthew 26:17-29; Mark 14:12-25; Luke 22:7-38).

The Passover was the Jewish remembrance of God's great deliverance of their nation from slavery in Egypt. The event celebrated God's mighty act of passing over all of those who had put the blood of a lamb on their doors. They were the only ones saved from the plague which killed all the first born of Egypt (see Exodus 11 and 12). Passover is still celebrated in Jewish homes today. Christians recognize Christ as the fulfillment of the Old Testament practice based on the Apostle Paul's assertion as recorded in 1 Corinthians 5:7. Jesus Christ's sacrifice on the Cross and His resurrection provides the means of deliverance from eternal death and access to God for believers.

Even as He approached His own death, Jesus expressed His love for His disciples. Jesus knew (1) that His hour of death had come (cf. John 2:4; 7:30; 8:20); (2) that He had come from God His Father; and (3) that He was the Father's unique Son with authority over all things.

POINTS TO PONDER

1. *On what occasion did Jesus wash His disciples' feet? (John 13:1)*

2. *Describe Simon Peter's attitude toward foot washing? How did Jesus deal with Peter's attitude? (vv. 6-8)*

3. *What does Jesus call Himself, according to verses 13 and 14? What point does He make by washing the disciples' feet? (vv. 13-15)*

4. *What does Jesus promise to people who acknowledge His lordship and their servanthood? (vv. 16-17)*

5. *How will "outsiders" react when they see our love? (vv. 34-35)*

_____

_____

LESSON AT-A-GLANCE

1. *The divine action of humble service (John 13:1-8)*
2. *The divine example of humble service (vv. 12-17)*
3. *The divine command of love among disciples (vv. 34-35)*

EXPLORING THE MEANING

1. The divine action of humble service (John 13:1-8)
The disciples had been arguing among themselves about which of them was the greatest (Luke 22:24). As they entered the Upper Room for the Passover celebration, there evidently was no servant to wash their feet. They were dirty and uncomfortable. Even though the pitcher, water basin, and long linen cloth were all present, not one of the 12 would humble himself to do the dirty job. For to wash the feet of the rest was to declare oneself the servant of all, and that was precisely what each resolved that he would not do. They sat there looking at the table, looking at the ceiling, and arranging their dress. Not one would confess himself a bit inferior to the others by performing the slave's office of washing feet. Finally, the Lord Jesus got up from the table, picked up a towel and began to wash the disciples' feet. Jesus the Lord washed the feet of His proud and selfish disciples—to demonstrate the nature of true love.

2. The divine example of humble service (vv. 12-17)
If the Lord had not proceeded to speak the words recorded here, Bible students would still, no doubt, take Jesus' humble service of

foot-washing as an example. But our Lord intended to drive the lesson home to the 12 disciples. The proud, self-centered disciples needed to know about the true nature of love and service within the Christian community.

Jesus knew that the lesson of love expressed in humble service would be necessary for the church to exist and grow. Therefore, He explained His action so that they (and we) might see that spoken love must also be expressed.

After a discussion with Peter, who objected to the Lord washing his feet (verses 6-8), Jesus resumed His place at the table and said, "Do you know what I have done to you? You call me Teacher and Lord; and you are right, for so I am. If I then, your Lord and Teacher, have washed your feet, you also ought to wash one another's feet. For I have given you an example, that you also should do as I have done to you. Truly, truly, I say to you, a servant is not greater than his master; nor is he who is sent greater than he who sent him. If you know these things, blessed are you if you do them" (vv. 12-17, RSV).

Jesus does not rebuke His disciples with harsh words but asks them if they grasp the significance of His action for their own future actions. "Do you know…?" He says. The One of highest position—the Lord and Teacher—had humbled Himself to serve the needs of others. Not only is this an example, but it is also an act showing the true greatness of Jesus. He was, indeed, the Teacher of authority and truth; He was indeed the Lord who deserved obedience.

Jesus then argues, "If I *being the Lord and Teacher* have served you [in this act of foot-washing], how much more ought you to serve one another?" (v. 14 paraphrased). He shows them that His ideal of lordship is to serve—even as He was about to become the Suffering Servant on the Cross (see Isaiah 53). The one who claims to follow Jesus must be like Him and serve as the true expression of love and greatness.

We might ask: Should we, as Jesus' disciples, practice actual foot-washing today? Though some do and experience great blessing from such action, the Scriptures do not seem to indicate that Jesus was establishing an ordinance, like baptism or the Lord's Supper.

He is not commanding the disciples to do *what* He has done but *as* He has done. In other words, His action is an example—one of many possible actions—of showing the humble service of love. To do *as* Jesus did means we must have the inner attitude of humility and love that moves us to perform actions that truly serve our Christian brothers and sisters. Jesus is our example. We must ask Him how we can express our service today.

3. The divine command of love among disciples (vv. 34-35)

The "new" command that Jesus gave is not unknown in the Old Testament (Leviticus 19:18) or in ethical literature. It is new in terms of its freshness, beauty, and desirability—the command to love has never become worn out or marred throughout the ages.

Jesus' command is new in another sense. The newness of the precept is set forth here in the sense that Jesus requires that His disciples shall love one another as *he loved them! His example* of constant, self-sacrificing love must be their attitude and pattern for relating toward one another. The kind of love which goes to the extreme (see John 13:1), serves with a humble spirit (v. 5), and eventually dies a sacrificial death for undeserving sinners, is the kind of love Jesus commands for His disciples.

You may wonder how love can be commanded. Perhaps we could best understand it as a precept—a guideline for life. For love is not an attitude or feeling. Love is a matter of the will.

Love seeks and acts in the best interest of the other person. The Lord showed His disciples this kind of love by washing their feet. Love, therefore, can be properly commanded if understood as an action. Feelings may come with or after the action, but the feelings must never be confused with *agape*, the self-sacrificing love spoken of here.

In verse 34, the command is repeated. No doubt, this is done to stress its importance for the spiritual welfare of all the church. Jesus goes on to explain that love among the disciples is also important to the non-Christian world: "By this all men will know that you are my disciples, if you have love for one another" (v. 35, RSV). Love is the identifying trait for Christian brothers and sisters. Attitudes of selfishness and bitterness among Christians deny the Lordship of Jesus Christ and cause unbelievers to mock and ridicule His name. We must go on obeying this commandment of love to honor our Lord, who loved us so much that He gave Himself to us.

DISCERNING MY DUTY

1. *Give concrete examples of how we can show the love of Christ in our relationships?*
2. *How should we interpret Christ's example of washing His disciples' feet?*
3. *What is true greatness according to Jesus?*

DECIDING MY RESPONSE

1. *How would the "foot-washing" principle of humble, loving service work: a) between employers and employees in a Christian business? b) among pastor and deacons (or stewards), and trustees?*

c) between the tenants and the building superintendent or owner?
d) between the president and his cabinet members?
2. Can this principle work outside of the Christian church and home? Why or why not?

This week, do something for at least one person in your church or on your job to express your love by an act of humble service.

LIGHT ON THE HEAVY

Foot-Washing. A hospitable amenity in Palestine, extended to guests upon arrival at the home of their host. It was usually performed by a servant, or by the wife of the host, while the guests were reclining at the table (Luke 7:44).

John relates that Jesus performed this menial service for His disciples at the Last Supper (John 13:4) as an example of the humble ministry they must ever be ready to perform for one another. The incident is an acted parable of His teaching: "Whoever would be great among you must be your servant, and whoever would be first among you must be slave of all" (Mark 10:43-44 and parallels). John undoubtedly intended the narrative to convey more than a lesson in humility. It was a sign of the entirely selfless love of Jesus that took Him to the humiliation of the Cross (cf. John 13:1). Many commentators also believe John considered foot-washing to be similar to the sacraments of baptism and the Eucharist, which symbolize how Christians are cleansed of the defilement of sin and nurtured in a communion of love with their Lord and one another.

The service of foot-washing of the "saints" is mentioned in 1 Timothy 5:10 among the qualifications of the order of widows. The ceremonial washing of feet in the church's liturgy is first attested about A.D. 400 by Augustine in connection with the Easter baptisms in certain churches. The earliest trace of the ceremony on Maundy Thursday—a custom continued in many churches to the present day—is in the seventh-century liturgy of the church in Spain (*The Interpreter's Dictionary of the Bible*, Vol. 2, Abingdon Press, Nashville, 1962, p. 308).

Teaching About Priorities
Based on Luke 12:13-40

DEFINING THE ISSUE

I do not want to be anywhere I would not want to be when Jesus comes.

I do not want to say anything I would not want to be saying when Jesus comes.

I do not want to do anything I would not want to be doing when Jesus comes.

There was a time when thousands of Americans tuned their television to watch J. R. Ewing plot, plan, and scheme his way through life. In one episode, J. R. set out to gain complete control of Ewing Oil, the family business. In the course of this one show, he cheated his brother Ray, blackmailed his brother Bobby, threatened his niece Lucy, and lied to his mother and ex-wife. J. R. used both family and "friends" in his effort to gain more power. You didn't have to watch the show very many times before you knew who was number one on J. R.'s list of priorities—J. R. Ewing.

Like J.R., the man in Christ's parable is already an extremely wealthy man (Luke 12:16). Yet his wealth still isn't enough. He saves what he has and sets up a new scheme to gain more. Both

J. R. and the "rich man" in this parable have priority problems. They use people to get things, instead of using things to benefit people. There is no room in their lives for anyone other than themselves.

Luke 12 records three parables that focus on "priority-setting." An examination of these parables reveals how Christians should establish and maintain their priorities in life.

AIM

By the end of the class, participants will have explored Jesus' teaching regarding priorities, will become convinced of the need to establish priorities in their own lives, evaluate their activities for the coming week, and determine to give God His rightful place in their endeavors.

SCRIPTURE TEXT

> LUKE 12:13 And one of the company said unto him, Master, speak to my brother, that he divide the inheritance with me.
>
> 14 And he said unto him, Man, who made me a judge or a divider over you?
>
> 15 And he said unto them, Take heed, and beware of covetousness: for a man's life consisteth not in the abundance of the things which he possesseth.
>
> 16 And he spake a parable unto them, saying, The ground of a certain rich man brought forth plentifully:
>
> 17 And he thought within himself, saying, What shall I do, because I have no room where to bestow my fruits?

18 And he said, This will I do: I will pull down my barns, and build greater; and there will I bestow all my fruits and my goods.

19 And I will say to my soul, Soul, thou hast much goods laid up for many years; take thine ease, eat, drink, and be merry.

20 But God said unto him, Thou fool, this night thy soul shall be required of thee: then whose shall those things be, which thou hast provided?

21 So is he that layeth up treasure for himself, and is not rich toward God.

35 Let your loins be girded about, and your lights burning;

36 And ye yourselves like unto men that wait for their lord, when he will return from the wedding; that when he cometh and knocketh, they may open unto him immediately.

37 Blessed are those servants, whom the lord when he cometh shall find watching: verily I say unto you, that he shall gird himself, and make them to sit down to meat, and will come forth and serve them.

38 And if he shall come in the second watch, or come in the third watch, and find them so, blessed are those servants.

39 And this know, that if the goodman of the house had known what hour the thief would come, he would have watched, and not have suffered his house to be broken through.

40 Be ye therefore ready also: for the Son of man cometh at an hour when ye think not.

BIBLE BACKGROUND

As Jesus' popularity with the common people grew, the scribes and Pharisees became more resentful and eventually plotted to get rid of Him. The hostility of the Pharisees accelerated as time went on, and Jesus did not hesitate to turn the searchlight on them to point out their duplicity. Luke 11 records Jesus' pronuncation of woes on them because of their hypocrisy and deception of people. In the midst of these teachings about hypocrisy, great crowds gathered. Though Jesus was ever mindful of the hunger and pain of the common people, He also realized He must never let their enthusiasm deter Him from His mission which was to give His life a ransom for many (Mark 10:45).

Jesus took the opportunity to warn His disciples of the coming persecution they would experience from the religious community, assuring them that God would be aware of their circumstances and would sustain them (Luke 12:4-7). While giving these instructions concerning what to expect in coming days, Jesus was interrupted by a man imploring him to settle a dispute he was having with his brother.

POINTS TO PONDER

1. *Why does Jesus warn us to be on guard against all kinds of greed? (Luke 12:15)*

   _____

   _____

2. *What was the rich man's solution to his problem of a lack of storage space? (v. 18)*

   _____

   _____

3. *How did he plan to spend his retirement years? (v. 19)*

4. *Why must we always be ready for Christ's return? (v. 40)*

THE LESSON AT-A-GLANCE

Jesus Teaches How to Establish and Maintain Priorities:

1. *Priority number one—do God's will (Luke 12:13-21)*
2. *Priority number two—maintain readiness (vv. 35-40)*
3. *Priority number three—help others get ready (Luke 16:15-16)*
4. *Priority test (Luke 12:31)*

EXPLORING THE MEANING

1. Priority number one—do God's will (Luke 12:13-21)
First of all, it is God's will that everyone believe and accept His Son Jesus Christ as personal Saviour (John 3:16).

Second, it is God's will that the believer first seek the kingdom of God and its righteousness (Luke 12:31).

The first two parables in our study this week concentrate on how covetousness prevents believers from seeking God's kingdom. Covetousness is defined in Webster's New Collegiate Dictionary as an inordinate desire for wealth or possessions or for another's possessions; having or showing a strong desire for possessions and especially for material possessions. Synonyms are greed, grasping, and avarice.

The Lord had just been discussing deep and holy matters and was perhaps still in the act of doing so (verses 1-12) when, without giving any sign that he had paid any attention to Jesus' words, a brother complained to Jesus that he wasn't getting enough money from his brother.

Some Bible scholars believe that the man's brother was wrong and that he appealed to Christ to correct the situation for him. Other scholars suggest that he wanted Christ to assist him in cheating his brother. The law stated that the older brother was entitled to a double portion of the estate (Deuteronomy 21:15-17). Some writers suggest that the brother wanted Christ to alter this law and make the elder brother divide the inheritance equally, and that the brother who made the request was not interested in justice, but possessions.

Whatever the brother's reason was, Jesus refused to become involved in this money squabble. Instead, Jesus used the opportunity to warn the young man, and the entire multitude, against covetousness. Jesus explained the proper priority of possessions in the life of the believer. Jesus warned believers to guard against greed (Luke 12:15). Greed is tricky. It can sneak into a believer's life and slowly take control until it eventually begins to choke out the love for God and others.

Why should believers eliminate the desire for "lots of things" from their lives? To present a clear picture of the results of covetousness, Jesus related the parable of the rich fool. Of the nearly 100 words in this parable, about 13 of them are "self-centered" words such as "I," "me," "mine," "my," and "myself." Not one other person seems to enter into the rich man's thoughts.

The man was "rich" (v. 16). He already possessed everything he could possibly need and most of the things he wanted. And yet, when he had another good crop and no room to store it, sharing with others less fortunate than himself never entered his mind.

The only solution he could find was to tear down his existing barns and build bigger ones to store more for "me."

When his new and bigger barns were built and full, he decided to take life easy. His number one priority was to do whatever brought pleasure to himself. "Take life easy; eat, drink, and be merry (v. 19)." Unfortunately, the cliche "eat, drink, and be merry for tomorrow we die" became true for him. God shocked him with the pronouncement, "You fool! This very night your life will be required from you. Then who will get what you have prepared for yourself?" (Luke 12:20, LB).

Scriptures warn never to call someone a fool unless we fully comprehend and mean what we are saying (i.e., Ecclesiastes 10:3, 14). God had some very good reasons for calling the rich man a fool.

A. The rich man *established* the wrong priorities. There was no room or time in his world for other people. People were only a means to an end, to be used to gain more wealth, possessions, and power for himself. Sharing what he had with God or others did not even appear on his list of priorities.

B. The rich man *maintained* the wrong priority. Although his priority was foolish, he was successful in maintaining it. But at what cost? He paid an extremely high price for his wealth and possessions. All of his wealth, power, possessions, and influence could not buy him even one extra minute of life. His dreams of just taking life easy and enjoying his wealth were shattered in one moment. When God demanded his life, he had nothing to show for the years he had spent on earth except a lot of "things."

Luke 12:15b "For a man's life does not consist in the abundance of his possessions." This true statement destroys one of the most widely accepted myths of our day. Many people seem to believe that the more they have, the less concern they need to have for their future. Christ says that security does not come from vast wealth. "Man shall not live by bread alone," Jesus told the tempter, "but by every word that proceeds from the mouth of God" (Matthew 4:4).

The rich man did not learn this truth until it was too late. He felt safe and secure after building his new barns and filling them with all his riches. But his safety and security existed only in his imagination. One's life is made secure not by things, but by triumph over love of things.

Have you established some priorities? Is doing God's will your number one priority?

2. Priority number two—maintain readiness (vv. 35-40)

Jesus further emphasizes proper priority-setting by relating a parable about a bridegroom. To fully understand this parable, the reader must understand that because the Eastern garment was long and flowing, the wearer had to tuck the skirts of his robe into his belt to allow freedom of motion. Lamps were kindled by live coals since matches were not yet invented. The Oriental groom, after a supper with his friends, went to the house of the bride to claim her. Since the return procession took place late at night, the groom expected his servants to be dressed for work and have their lamps lighted (*The Wycliffe Bible Commentary*, p. 1050).

The traditional wedding preparation was an illustration of the believer's readiness for the return of Jesus Christ. The change of figure from the bridegroom to the thief (v. 39) emphasized the element of surprise in Christ's unexpected appearance. Paul used this same figure of speech to describe the Lord's second coming (1 Thessalonians 5:2).

A well-known minister tells a story about how his father often told the older children of the family to clean the house. When they asked him, "Are we going to have company?" He would explain that while they weren't expecting anyone to come, they should be ready, just in case."

Instead of having an emergency plan put into effect when we think our Lord's return is near, believers should always be ready. While the servants waited for the bridegroom, they dressed for work and trimmed lamps. What are believers to do as they wait for the coming of Christ?

3. Priority number three—helping others to get ready (Luke 16:15-16)

It is God's will that we not only get ourselves ready for His coming, but that we also help others to get ready.

Have you ever had the experience of planning a jam-packed vacation only to look back when it was over and wondering where the time went? The anticipated hours of relaxation eluded you. The important things you had planned to do became swallowed up by the immediate things. Planned priorities had to take second place to the urgent priorities.

The Prophet Jeremiah describes a similar situation, but with dire results: "The harvest is finished, the summer is ended, and we are not saved" (Jeremiah 8:20, LB). Poor judgment has been shown in giving priority to lesser things.

Some Christians seem to feel that their spirituality is measured by the number of activities they engage in. They wind themselves up like mechanical toys and let themselves "go." Often the "going" is without purpose or plan. Some other believers feel their self-worth is determined by the number of church activities in which they participate. The busier they are, the better they feel about themselves. Still others are quite willing to let the 20 percent of the congregation do 80 percent of the work while they themselves are content with their own priorities.

4. Priority Test (Luke 31)

The Christian believer lives in a world where numerous concerns must be evaluated and prioritized. These areas typically relate to God, self, family, church, employment, and community. Time must be allocated for each activity. While the amount of time will vary from person to person, relating to God through personal devotions and corporate (church) worship ought to be at the top of the list. Often, employment hours are dictated by the employer. Time spent with family members—spouse, children, etc.—should be high on the list. In fact, establishing a list of one's priorities, whether by fixing them in one's mind or by writing them down, is an important part of keeping the proper balance.

Jesus' warning to the rich man is intended for us today. As we sort out the priorities for our lives, we should pay close attention to this warning. We do not want to make the fatal mistake he made.

DISCERNING MY DUTY

1. *Why should believers distinguish between life's necessities and the urge to have "lots of things"?*
2. *Have you established some priorities? Is doing God's will your number one priority?*
3. *Instead of having an emergency plan put into effect when we think our Lord's return is near, how should believers live?*
4. *What are some sound principles believers should follow as they wait for the coming of Christ?*

DECIDING MY RESPONSE

List several (at least five) major activities scheduled for the week. Prioritize these activities taking into account your responsibility to God, self, spouse (if any), children, church, employment, and community. Ask God to give you wisdom in developing your list so you will give highest priority to those areas which are of greatest concern to Him.

LIGHT ON THE HEAVY

Inheritance. Jewish custom had a law of inheritance, which dictated that land belonged to the family rather than to the individual. The eldest son received a double portion and the others equal shares. If a man died, leaving no sons, the inheritance passed to his daughters; if no daughters, to his brothers; if no brothers, to his father's brothers or to the next of kin.

Parables. The word parable is derived from the Greek word parabole, which literally means putting things side by side. Parables were used as a form of teaching which presented the listener with interesting illustrations from which moral and religious truths could be drawn. Jesus' parables were not merely illustrations of general principles, but they embodied messages which could not be as effectively conveyed any other way.

They were an appropriate form of communication for bringing out the message of the kingdom. Sometimes the lesson of a parable was quite obvious from the story itself, as in the story of the rich fool, where the rich man died at the very moment he had completed his preparation to retire in security and comfort.(*New Bible Dictionary*, edited by I. Howard Marshall, A.R. Millard, J.I. Packer, D.J. Wiseman. Downers Grove: Inter-Varsity Press, 1996, pp. 505-6, 867-9).

MORE LIGHT ON THE TEXT

The first 12 verses of Luke chapter 12 are a series of warnings and encouragements Jesus spoke to his disciples and the multitude that gathered to hear. He warned against the hypocrisy of the Pharisees who tried to conceal their true nature, and said that such cover-ups would be revealed (vv.1-3). In verses 4-9, he encouraged them not to be afraid of man, but to fear God, who controlled the final destiny of man. Man can kill the mortal body, but it is God who has the power to kill and put into hell's fire. God is the only one we should fear.

Jesus warned them about the seriousness and consequences of blaspheming the Holy Spirit which, he said, was the unpardonable sin (v. 10). He explained that speaking against the Son of man is pardonable, but speaking against the Holy Spirit is unpardonable. He then assured them of the presence of the Holy Spirit when they appeared before authorities to be judged. Therefore, they did not need to panic, thinking how to defend themselves; rather, they should rely on the Holy Spirit who would teach them what to say when the time came (vv. 11-12).

Luke 12:13 And one of the company said unto him, Master, speak to my brother, that he divide the inheritance with me. 14 And He said unto him, Man, who made me a judge or divider over you?

As he was speaking, one of the people in the crowd came to him and made a request, and Jesus seized the opportunity to teach a very fundamental lesson on the futility of acquiring wealth at the expense of the knowledge of God. The conjunction "And" (kai) serves as a transition from the previous thought to a new one. Verse 1 tells us that the number that gathered to hear him was countless. The crowd was so large (probably many thousands,

NIV) that they were trampling on one another. Perhaps it could be described as a stampede.

From this crowd came one person who asked Jesus to help settle a family dispute about an inheritance. He asked Jesus to tell his brother (his older brother) to divide the inheritance. According to Jewish tradition, the first son in a family is given preference in the distribution of the family inheritance when the father dies. He is entitled to a double share of the entire family inheritance (compare Deuteronomy 21:15-17). This is included in the law that governed marriage among the Jewish people.

This is consistent with the tradition in many parts of Nigeria, especially among the Igbos. If a man has more than one wife (two or three) and the wives each have children, the first male child takes over all the father's inheritance when the father dies. He administers the father's property and shares it among his brethren. If there are three sons in the family, for example, the inheritance is divided into two equal parts. The first takes one half of his choice and the second half is shared among the rest of the sons in the family, according to their ages, with preference given to the older ones. If there are only two sons, the first takes two-thirds. Dispute of the nature described in this passage is reminiscent of what happens among the Igbos.

We are concerned mainly about Jesus' action or reaction in this case. We notice that the man called Jesus Master (Greek *didaskalos*) teacher, which is equivalent to the Hebrew Rabbi. Rabbis have the ability to interpret the law. Thus, the inquirer approached Jesus to render judgment. What made him turn to Jesus for help? We can only speculate. The vast knowledge and authority with which Jesus was teaching might have prompted him, or it is possible that he was motivated by Christ's mention of legal matters in the previous verse and, therefore, decided to bring the family matter to Jesus. However, Jesus refused to get involved in this domestic dispute, not because of an inability to answer, or a lack of concern for social and ethical matters, but because it was not the concern of the kingdom of God. He answered by asking the man a rhetorical question: "Who made me a judge or a divider over you?" In doing so, Jesus focused on another important, and often hidden, area of human character—motive.

15 And said unto them, Take heed, and beware of covetousness: for a man's life consisteth not in the abundance of the things which he possesseth.
After the short dialogue with the man, Jesus turned to the crowd and cautioned them, "Take heed, and beware of covetousness." The phrase "take heed" (Greek *horate)* means to be watchful and "beware" (Greek *phulassesde*) from the verb *phulasso* to be on guard; keep or preserve oneself. The warning can be rephrased thus: Watch yourselves (or watch out) and be on your guard (be careful) lest the spirit of covetousness rule your hearts.

The word "covetousness" is the translation of the Greek compound word *pleonexia*, which means ruthless greed; a grasping after the most and the best without regard of others. This is an attitude of selfish desire to take what does not rightly belong to you or wanting to take another person's things. Covetousness leads to all types of evil. This type of sin led Ahab to take Naboth's land and kill him. It also led David to take Uriah's wife and kill him. The Bible forbids and condemns covetousness in several passages (See Exodus 20:17; Matthew 6:19-21; Ephesians 5:3). Covetousness can also be discontentment or dissatisfaction with what one has (Hebrews 13:5), which can lead to the desire for, and pursuit of, more and more earthly things.

Jesus advanced this caution with the explanation that "a man's life consisteth not in the abundance of the things which he possesseth" (v. 15b). In other words, our joy, happiness, or comfort does not depend on the amount of wealth we have acquired in this world. Jesus said that the accumulation of wealth should not become the motive, or main goal, for our life in this world.

16 And he spake a parable unto them, saying, The ground of a certain rich man brought forth plentifully: 17 And he thought within himself, saying, What shall I do, because I have no room where to bestow my fruits?

Jesus, then, illustrated His point with a parable, as was His custom. The parable was intended to dramatize the danger of covetousness and demonstrate that life does not consist of earthly possessions. This parable was the story about the life and death of a rich man who occupied himself with worldly gratification based on wealth. It allows us to judge whether he was a happy man or not.

According to Jesus, the man was a farmer who had a "bumper crop" for the year, i.e., his land "brought forth plentifully." The harvest was good. His crop was so bountiful that he did not have enough room in his barn to store it. He ran out of space. Jesus' use of a farmer to illustrate this point is important. Farming was the most common occupation of the Jews. Therefore, Jesus used an illustration that the people could understand best and relate to easily.

Overwhelmed with such bounty, the farmer thought that he would accumulate and preserve for himself all the harvest that he could. The word translated "thought" here is the Greek word *dielogizeto* which means to debate, to deliberate, cast in mind, or dispute. The idea is that he agonized or debated within himself in such a way that it became of great concern to him. In translation, "he thought" fails to give us any wrong idea of the turmoil that went through his mind as he debated what to do with such a plentiful harvest. He must have spent days and sleepless nights thinking about what to do. In his anxiety and desperation, he asked himself, "What shall I do (now)?"

18 And, he said, This will I do: I will pull down my barns, and build greater; and there will I bestow all my fruits and my goods. 19 And will say to my soul, Soul, thou hast much goods laid up for many years; take ease, eat, and drink and be merry. After worrying about what he should do with his harvest, the farmer finally came up with a solution. He resolved within himself, "I will pull down my barns, and build greater." Notice how an egotistical attitude of greed and selfishness is clearly revealed by the use of the first-person singular pronouns "I" and "my" in these two verses. The two pronouns appear seven times (implicitly nine) in this section. A greedy, covetous, and selfish person thinks only about himself and his well-being, and neglects others. He often gratifies himself at the expense of others. The rich "fool" as he is generally referred to (v. 20), was so self-absorbed that he never thought of any other way to resolve the problem, other than hoarding the goods for himself. He never thought of the poor or underprivileged in his neighborhood, who might need some help. He was also foolish in thinking that the future was under his control and not in God's hands.

We see a picture of misplaced confidence. Instead of relying on God for "tomorrow," he placed his confidence in himself; and instead of giving thanks to God for the good harvest, he took the credit himself. Instead of looking for a way to use his goods wisely, and to honor God by helping people, he selfishly hoarded the goods. He did not take into account that "the earth is the Lord's and everything in it" (Psalm 24:1-2, NIV). God owns "the cattle on a thousand hills" (Psalm 50:10, NIV), and it is God who gives rain to water the fields that produce the crops (Job 5:10, LB). He planned his own life and said to himself, "Relax, have fun, and enjoy yourself for you have good things stored up that will last for many years to come." But he was unaware of what God had planned for him.

20 God said unto him, Thou fool, this night thy soul shall be required of thee: then whose shall those things be, which thou hast provided?
The scene now changes from man to God. It is now God's turn to talk. God speaks to him and calls him a "fool" (Greek *aphron*), which means senseless person; stupid or one acting unintelligently. The Psalmist also calls any person who says there is no God, "a fool" (Psalm 14:1-2). Paul advises the Ephesian Christians, "Do not be fools, but understand what the Lord's will is" (Ephesians 5:17). The man in this parable neither recognized God's existence, nor discerned God's will for him.

That night, as the man contemplated how he was going to enjoy himself for years to come, God came to pronounce judgment upon him. God said, "This night thy soul shall be required of thee," that means death. The Greek phrase *taute te vukti* (literally, this the night), which the KJV translates "this night" is better rendered "this very night" (NIV). This translation denotes the seriousness and urgency of the matter.

The word "required," is the Greek word translated *apaiteo*, which means to demand back or ask again. Man has no control over his life. All life belongs to God, the Creator. The sentence could read, "This very night, your soul (life) is demanded," or "I demand your life this very night." This implies that he had no choice and clearly described a true picture of the helplessness and lack of control he had over his own life.

The question that follows, "Then whose shall those things be, which thou hast provided?" made the point clear. God seems to ask him, "Now that you are going to die, to whom are you going to leave all the wealth you have accumulated?" Of course, God was not expecting an answer, but the question seemed to ridicule the man who foolishly put his mind on worldly riches, without being rich toward God.

21 So is he that layeth up treasure for himself, and is not rich toward God.

Jesus gave an explanation of this parable in verse 21: A man who gives priority to storing treasure for himself is not rich at all, if he is not rich in God. He also warned against trusting in riches earlier in His teachings: "Do not store up for yourselves treasures on earth, where moth and rust destroy, and where thieves break in and steal. But store up for yourselves treasures in heaven, where moth and rust do not destroy, and where thieves do not break in and steal. For where your treasure is, there your heart will be also" (Matthew 6:19-21, NIV). Therefore, we should make it our priority to seek first God's kingdom and His righteousness, and every other thing will be "added unto you" (Matthew 6:33).

Reversing the World's Standard
Based on Matthew 18:1-4; 20:17-28

DEFINING THE ISSUE

Many recognize Nelson Rolihlahia Mandela as the first Black president of South Africa. Yet few comprehend that his greatness resulted from servanthood and suffering for human rights. Mandela, a son of a Tembu tribe in Umtata, became a lawyer and a member of the African National Congress. He knew that apartheid was wrong and fought against it.

Mandela was arrested in August 1962 for treason and sentenced to life imprisonment in June 1964 for sabotage and treason. Although he was innocent of both counts, Mandela spent over 27 years in prison. Words can't describe Mandela's suffering during these many years. But his perseverance and God's reversal of the world's standard would prevail. In February 1990, President F.W. DeKlerk released Mandela from prison.

Mandela served his country by assuming leadership of the African National Congress. In 1991, the South African government repealed the last of the laws that formed the legal basis for "apartheid." Mandela was recognized with President DeKlerk and they received the 1993 Nobel Peace Prize for their efforts in establishing democracy and racial harmony in South Africa. From suffering and servanthood, Nelson Rolihlahia Mandela was elected the first black president of South Africa in 1994. This was the first national election in which blacks could vote.

Mandela's life is a true example of how God's standards are different than the world's standard for greatness. The White South African government in 1962 never could have comprehended that the man they imprisoned and framed for treason would become president of their country in 1994. Man's ways are not God's ways. This lesson, however, will further explain how obtaining greatness in God's kingdom is different from how one obtains greatness in the world.

AIM

By the end of the lesson, participants will describe the difference between the world's standard and God's standard of greatness; they will desire His standard of greatness for themselves and seek to develop God's standard of greatness for their lives instead of the world's standard.

SCRIPTURE TEXT

> MATTHEW 18:1 At the same time came the disciples unto Jesus, saying, Who is the greatest in the kingdom of heaven?
>
> 2 And Jesus called a little child unto him, and set him in the midst of them,
>
> 3 And said, Verily I say unto you, Except ye be converted, and become as little children, ye shall not enter into the kingdom of heaven.
>
> 4 Whosoever therefore shall humble himself as this little child, the same is greatest in the kingdom of heaven.

MATTHEW 20:17 And Jesus going up to Jerusalem took the twelve disciples apart in the way, and said unto them,

18 Behold, we go up to Jerusalem; and the Son of man shall be betrayed unto the chief priests and unto the scribes, and they shall condemn him to death,

19 And shall deliver him to the Gentiles to mock, and to scourge, and to crucify him: and the third day he shall rise again.

20 Then came to him the mother of Zebedee's children with her sons, worshipping him, and desiring a certain thing of him.

21 And he said unto her, What wilt thou? She saith unto him, Grant that these my two sons may sit, the one on thy right hand, and the other on the left, in thy kingdom.

22 But Jesus answered and said, Ye know not what ye ask. Are ye able to drink of the cup that I shall drink of, and to be baptized with the baptism that I am baptized with? They say unto him, We are able.

23 And he saith unto them, Ye shall drink indeed of my cup, and be baptized with the baptism that I am baptized with: but to sit on my right hand, and on my left, is not mine to give, but it shall be given to them for whom it is prepared of my Father.

24 And when the ten heard it, they were moved with indignation against the two brethren.

25 But Jesus called them unto him, and said, Ye know that the princes of the Gentiles exercise dominion over

them, and they that are great exercise authority upon them.

26 But it shall not be so among you: but whosoever will be great among you, let him be your minister;

27 And whosoever will be chief among you, let him be your servant:

28 Even as the Son of man came not to be ministered unto, but to minister, and to give his life a ransom for many.

BIBLE BACKGROUND

The gospel of Matthew has five discourses in which Jesus dialogues with the disciples and the multitudes of people. Matthew 18 and 20 are part of the fourth discourse in the five presented. In the fourth discourse, Jesus taught many principles about the Christian community and how it should operate. He began this teaching soon after arriving in Capernaum with the disciples. The disciples had been disputing among themselves, while traveling to Capernaum, about who was the greatest (Mark 9:34). Jesus was compelled to answer them and, if He answered them, perhaps He could put an end to their dispute.

Despite Jesus' answer concerning the requirements for greatness in God's kingdom, the disciples were still occupied with the question about who would be the greatest, and who would sit on the right and the left of Jesus. Their great concern about their position in the kingdom stemmed from the belief that the coming of Jesus Christ meant He was about to establish His kingdom and throw off Roman rule. Jesus himself had proclaimed that the kingdom was at hand, but they had misunderstood the nature of the kingdom for that time.

POINTS TO PONDER

1. *What did Jesus do to illustrate "Who is the greatest in the kingdom of heaven?" (Matthew 18:2)*

   _____
   _____

2. *What did Jesus foretell to the disciples as they traveled to Jerusalem? (Matthew 20:18-19)*

   _____
   _____

3. *How did Jesus reply to James' and John's mother concerning their status in God's kingdom? (v. 22)*

   _____
   _____

4. *Why did Jesus have to call the other disciples aside and further explain about greatness in God's kingdom? (vv. 24-28)*

   _____
   _____

LESSON AT-A-GLANCE

1. *Greatness Requires Humility (Matthew 18:1-4)*
2. *Greatness Requires Dying to Self (Matthew 20:17-19)*
3. *Greatness Requires Suffering (vv. 20-23)*
4. *Greatness Requires Servanthood (vv. 24-28)*

EXPLORING THE MEANING

1. Greatness Requires Humility (Matthew 18:1-4)

Man's nature craves greatness. The disciples were no exception. They sought greatness in God's kingdom. Greatness in God's kingdom requires a different standard than the world's standard. Greatness by the world's standard involves wealth, power, and status. God's kingdom reverses the world's standard for greatness. The disciples would soon learn about this standard reversal.

In the midst of the disciples' time with Jesus, they began a dispute over who would be the greatest in God's kingdom. The disciples knew that the Messiah would set up a kingdom, God's kingdom. And Jesus had already taught them that there would be distinctions in the kingdom (Matthew 5:19). Therefore, they brought the question to Jesus: "Who is the greatest in the kingdom of heaven?" (Matthew 18:1).

Jesus, being the greatest Teacher ever, illustrated the answer by calling a child to himself. Children were drawn to Jesus' tenderness. They did not fear Him. Once the child was in their midst, He stated: "Verily I say unto you, Except ye be converted, and become as little children, ye shall not enter into the kingdom of heaven. Whosoever therefore shall humble himself as this little child, the same is greatest in the kingdom of heaven" (vv. 3-4). Jesus' statement, "Verily, I say unto you" is often translated as "I tell you the truth." This statement emphasizes what Jesus is about to say must be taken seriously and be obeyed.

Jesus said, "Except ye be converted," meaning that there must be a change or a turnaround within them. It implied that one must turn from one's self and change one's course of conduct. This did mean that they weren't Christians and needed to be converted. Yet their hearts must be changed to that of a little child. Little children are free of ambition, pride, and haughtiness. They are typically humble and teachable. The disciples' hearts, in order to be changed, must be full of humility, free from worldly ambition, and free from the lust of power, if they desired greatness in God's kingdom.

God's kingdom reverses the world's standard for greatness. Unlike the world, humility characterizes greatness in God's kingdom, more important than ability, achievement, and performance. A child's humility is an ideal example of God's standard for greatness. For a child's mind is one of humility, with little concern for social status. The child's humility consists of an attitude of trust and dependence on adults. This humility must be manifested in one's life in order to be considered great in God's kingdom.

2. Greatness Requires Dying to Self (Matthew 20:17-19)
The disciples believed that Jesus was their great Messiah, yet they didn't comprehend that His greatness would involve death on the cross. As Jesus prepared to enter Jerusalem for the last time, He took the 12 disciples aside to explain, for the third time, what His messiahship involved (See Matthew 16:21-23; 17:9,22-23). It was necessary for Jesus to take the disciples aside from the crowd, in order to communicate with them what others could not hear or understand.

Jesus' great messiahship required His death on the cross, which would occur during this trip to Jerusalem. Jesus, therefore, explained to the disciples that they were going into Jerusalem and that the Son of Man would be betrayed (v. 18). He would be betrayed by Judas and delivered to the chief priests and scribes. They would condemn Him to death and turn Him over to the Gentiles. The Gentiles were the Roman authorities who had the right to execute punishment of mocking, flogging, and crucifixion. Although the Jews condemned Jesus to death, the punishment of the cross was Roman, not Jewish.

Jesus' greatness was demonstrated by His willingness to die on the cross and highlighted by His resurrection. Jesus not only predicted His crucifixion, but also His resurrection on the third day

(v. 19). Jesus' prediction of His resurrection was not understood by the disciples. His greatness required His death and resurrection for all mankind.

3. Greatness Requires Suffering (vv. 20-23)

The concept of greatness in God's kingdom was continually on the minds of the disciples and others. Even after Jesus predicted His death and resurrection, the mother of two of the disciples' approached Jesus concerning her sons' position in God's kingdom. Salome, the mother of Zebedee's sons, James and John, requested a favor from Jesus (v. 20). She approached Jesus with full respect by kneeling down before Him.

Salome requested that her sons, James and John, be given greatness in God's kingdom, by way of a seating position. Salome, along with many others, were expecting Jesus to set up an earthly kingdom. They expected Him to conquer and reign on earth. And, when this would occur, Salome desired that her sons be given the places of highest honor, on Jesus' right and on His left.

She asked, "Grant that these my two sons may sit, the one on thy right hand, and the other on the left, in thy kingdom."

The "right hand" and the "left hand," suggest proximity to Jesus and a share in His prestige and power. John, James, and their mother desired that they might share in the authority and preeminence of Jesus the Messiah, when His kingdom is fully consummated.

Jesus' answer to their request confirms that humans cannot comprehend what greatness in God's kingdom requires. Jesus said, "Ye know not what ye ask. Are ye able to drink of the cup that I shall drink of, and to be baptized with the baptism that I am baptized with?" (v. 22). He was clearly stating that if one desired greatness in God's kingdom, one must be ready to drink from the same cup of suffering. Jesus was the Suffering Savior, and in order to be baptized or identified with Him, one must identify with the suffering. Although James and John couldn't comprehend what Jesus was saying, they quickly answered, "We are able." (v. 22b).

Jesus replied to their hasty answer by stating, "Ye shall drink indeed of my cup, and be baptized with the baptism that I am baptized with: but to sit on my right hand, and on my left, is not mine to give, but it shall be given to them for whom it is prepared of my Father" (v. 23). He knew the suffering that the disciples and others would undergo for His sake. Tradition has it that both James and John identified with Jesus' suffering. James was the first of the apostles to be martyred (Acts 12:2), and John suffered exile on the Isle of Patmos during his last days (Revelation 1:9). Despite the suffering James, John, and others would endure, Jesus made it clear that greatness in God's kingdom was not His to determine. For God has prepared the rewards for those whom He has chosen. The position on the right and left of Jesus has already been assigned by the Father. Jesus cannot assign anything upon a mother's request.

4. Greatness Requires Servanthood (vv. 24-28)

It is quite evident that, despite the previous discussion (Matthew 18:1-4), the disciples did not understand the standard for greatness in God's kingdom. The remaining 10 disciples were angry upon hearing about Salome's, James', and John's request (v. 24). They had forgotten Jesus' illustration concerning greatness and childlike humility. Jesus had to call them together to further explain what greatness in God's kingdom involved.

First, He reminded them of how the Gentile rulers exercised their greatness on earth by lording their authority over others (v. 25). But this was not to be true among believers and in God's kingdom. Greatness in God's kingdom is derived from service. If one desires to be great before God, one must be willing to serve. To be great or first in God's kingdom, one must become a slave (v. 27). Yet by the world's standard, one cannot imagine a slave being given leadership.

Second, this principle of servanthood must be applied here on earth. Those who want to be great among God's people, must learn first how to serve here on earth. A servant is one of the lowest positions a man can have on earth, yet Jesus said that we must learn to be servants to one another. Only as we become servants can we find ourselves honored and promoted.

Finally, Jesus presented Himself as the supreme example of service to others. Jesus was in the form of God in heaven; yet He came to earth as a humble child in earthly life. He did not come to earth to be served by people, but to serve them. He demonstrated the ultimate servanthood by "giving his life a ransom for many" (v. 28). Jesus died for all sinners. And we are all sinners. He became the "atonement" for all. Although only ONE died, many find their lives "ransomed, healed, restored, forgiven." Jesus is, therefore, the ultimate example of greatness through humility, death, suffering, and servanthood.

DISCERNING MY DUTY

1. *What did Jesus mean when he said that "one must change and become like a little child in order to enter God's kingdom?"*
2. *Do you think that James and John really understood Jesus when He asked, "Can you drink the cup I am going to drink?" Explain your answer.*
3. *Explain in your own words why Jesus said He came to serve and give His life as a ransom for many.*

DECIDING MY RESPONSE

The "homeless," those who are not able to provide shelter for themselves, are a great concern in our society. We don't know what to do with them, and many people look down on them. What about serving them? Is that being willing to help them in whatever way they need help? As Christians, we should humble ourselves and reach out to the "homeless" in our neighborhood. We need to be willing to serve them and not have an attitude of "being better than they." It is only by God's grace that we are not "homeless."

How many adults would be willing to follow a path leading to greatness if they had to follow the road of humility? Humility is a difficult characteristic to demonstrate in our daily lives. Yet we have an example of humility in the life of Christ. Read Philippians 2:1-11. Write down on a piece of paper three actions of Jesus that demonstrated humility. Then pray that God would show you three actions you can take next week to demonstrate humility. For example, maybe you can take out the trash at home every night this week without being told or receiving a compliment. Maybe you can offer to work in the nursery during the evening service or prayer meeting. Trust God to show you how to develop greatness through humility this next week.

LIGHT ON THE HEAVY

Salome. "Mother of the sons of Zebedee." She was James' and John's mother. Although she is known for asking Jesus to let her two sons sit on His right and on His left side, she was also one of the three women who observed the crucifixion and went to the tomb on Resurrection morning. Her husband was Zebedee.

Kingdom of Heaven. Also known as The Kingdom of God. The synoptic gospels approach the theme of the "Kingdom of heaven or God" as the central theme of Jesus' preaching. Matthew speaks of it as the "kingdom of heaven," while Mark and Luke speak of it as the "kingdom of God." In most instances both have the same meaning. The expression originates with the late Jewish expectation of the future which denotes a decisive intervention of God to restore His people's fortunes and liberate them from the power of their enemies. The coming of this kingdom is the great perspective of the future, prepared by the coming of the Messiah, which, as they see it, paves the way for the kingdom of God.

(*New Bible Dictionary*, edited by I. Howard Marshall, A.R. Millard, Packer, D.J. Wiseman. Inter-Varsity Press, Downers Grove, Illinois, 1996, pp. 1046, 647-50)

MORE LIGHT ON THE TEXT

Chapter 17 of the gospel of Matthew is an account of the transfiguration of Jesus (Matthew 17:1-13), the healing of the boy who was demon-possessed (vv. 14-23), and the dispute over paying tax to the temple (vv. 24-27). Chapter 18 contains a series of teachings regarding the kingdom of heaven, forgiveness, and the conditions for entering the kingdom. One of the conditions is humility. According to the world's standard, it looks illogical, but to Jesus, it is a great virtue for entrance into God's presence. In these passages, Matthew 18:1-4; 20:17-28, Jesus dramatically demonstrates that humility and service to others are the essence of life and the criteria for the kingdom of heaven.

Matthew 18:1 At the same time, came the disciples unto Jesus, saying, Who is the greatest in the kingdom of heaven? 2 And Jesus called a little child unto him, and set him in the midst of them.

Jesus and His disciples are in Capernaum. They have just paid their taxes in an unusual and miraculous way after being challenged by the authorities. Just then, the disciples ask Him the question about who would be greatest in the kingdom of heaven. "At the same time" (lit. "hour") seems to link the preceding incident concerning taxes. This seems to signify the sequence of the events (the paying of the taxes by Christ and His disciples, and the asking of the question), and the speed with which both events took place. One immediately follows the other. The phrase can be reworded, thus: "At the same moment." According to Mark's account of the story, Jesus and the disciples are in a house, probably Peter's (compare Mark 1:21,29), but Matthew omits the house. This seems to suggest that the question followed immediately after the tax incident, on the way, before they got to the house. Tax collectors have their booths along the streets to demand taxes (Mark 2:13ff), which further supports the idea that they paid their taxes before reaching the house.

What prompted the question? Matthew does not give us the answer. According to Mark 9:33-37, the disciples are disputing along the way to Capernaum about "who is the greatest." They keep quiet when Jesus challenges them. Luke 9:46-48 says that Jesus discerned their thoughts. We can only suggest a number of reasons that prompted the question and probably, as we shall see in Chapter 20, the question of "who is the greatest" seems to be a recurring issue among the disciples throughout the ministry of Jesus. The first suggestion is because Jesus had just taken only

Peter, James, and John to the mountaintop where they experienced the transfiguration (Matthew 17:1-3; Mark 9:2).

The second suggestion is that Peter had always been singled out, being the more vocal of the disciples (Matthew 14:28-29; 15:15; 16:16-18; 17:4), and James and John may have thought the greatest was Peter. In Matthew 5:19, Jesus said that there would be distinctions in the kingdom. These and other things set off the contention among them, which continues in the ambition of Zebedee's sons and their mother (Matthew 20:20-23; compare Mark 10:35-45). These events, coupled with the immediate incident of paying taxes, keep the disciples pondering who will be the greatest in heaven. Rank was an important and prominent issue within the Jewish community. That is why Jesus spoke on many occasions against the Pharisees. According to Matthew, they confront Jesus with the question, *Who is the greatest in the kingdom of heaven?* In answer to the question, Jesus uses a visual aid. He calls a little child and has the child stand in the midst of them.

3 Then said, Verily I say unto you, Except ye be converted, and become as little children, ye shall not enter into the kingdom of heaven. 4 Whosoever therefore shall humble himself as this little child, the same is greatest in the kingdom of heaven.
With the solemn introductory formula, "*Verily I say unto you,*" also used 27 times in Matthew, Jesus cautions His disciples that they need to "change and become like little children." If they do not, they will "not enter the kingdom of heaven." "Verily" (Greek *amen*), sometimes used doubled (verily, verily), means *surely*, and signifies the certainty, or seriousness, and the trustworthiness of what the speaker is about to say. Christ often uses this formula when giving an important teaching instruction that needs everyone's greatest attention. It is a way of saying, "I tell you the truth

(NIV), I am not lying to you." The word "converted" (Greek *strepho*) means to twist, i.e., to turn around or reverse, to turn oneself. It has the idea of change of direction. When we become Christians, we not only repent, and are sorry for our sins, but we make an about-face (turn around) and change our direction to walk with the Lord (Acts 3:19). From what are the disciples to turn? What does the child signify in the teaching? The answer to the first question is that they need to change their wrong attitude of inordinate ambition of being the greatest. To answer the second question, the child represents humility and trust. Jesus is not talking about innocence, faith, or purity of children, but He is advocating humility, which to Jewish people, and the world, is debasing. Jesus is saying that they should not follow the norm of society. Society desires ambition for fame, power, and honor (Matthew 23:5-12). To be like children, who do not have such worldly desires, is more in tune with what Jesus desires. Accordingly, the disciples are to change from their selfish ambition and pride and adopt a new norm of humility or be excluded from the kingdom of heaven. Conversely, the person who humbles (*tapeinosei*, i.e., "will humble") himself like "this little child, the same is greatest in the kingdom of heaven." Humility, to Jesus, is an honorable virtue and a condition for entrance into His kingdom. It is the foundation of character (Matthew 5:3, 5; 23:12; Luke 14:11; 18:14). But to the Greeks, humility is weak and contemptible. Paul emphasized the humility and subsequent exaltation of Jesus (See Philippians 2:1-11; 2 Corinthians 8:9), and commanded us to humble ourselves towards one another. (Philippians 2:3-4; Romans 12:10).

The "kingdom of heaven" is a term peculiar to Matthew, the equivalent to the "kingdom of God." It refers to the eternal future realm to be inaugurated by Christ's return, where Christ will reign eternally with those who have been redeemed by His blood. To enter it and to have a part in it eternally, one must be converted (v. 3; John 3:3).

20:17 And Jesus going up to Jerusalem took the twelve disciples apart in the way, and said unto them, 18 Behold, we go up to Jerusalem; and the Son of man shall be betrayed unto the chief priests and unto the scribes, and they shall condemn him to death, 19 And shall deliver him to the Gentiles to mock and to scourge, and to crucify him: and the third day he shall rise again.

Jesus and His disciples left the region of Galilee (Capernaum is a city in the region of Galilee) and went down toward the region of Judea (Matthew 19:1), where Jesus continued His teaching and was being followed by a large crowd. As they journeyed toward Jerusalem, He took His disciples (the 12) aside from among the crowd and began to tell them the purpose of their trip to Jerusalem. Jerusalem is the focal point of Jewish worship, and so it was customary for pilgrims to frequent Jerusalem. It was, therefore, not out of place for Jesus and His disciples to go to Jerusalem. However, this was an extraordinary trip, and Jesus knew that. He stopped on the way, called the 12 apart, and told them the main reason for the present trip into Jerusalem. He said that the Son of Man is to be betrayed and condemned to death.

Verses 18 and 19 describe in detail the sequence of events leading to the death of Christ. He will be betrayed to the chief priests and scribes (i.e., the Jewish religious hierarchy), who will consequently condemn Him to death through their illegal proceedings. They will hand Him over to the Gentiles (i.e., the Roman authorities) who will mock Him (Greek *empaizai*; i.e., ridicule Him), torture Him (by flogging Greek, *mastigosai*), and crucify (*staurosai*)

REVERSING THE WORLD'S STANDARD

Him (See Matthew 16:21; Acts 2:23). The news is not all "gloom and doom," however. Jesus seems to say, on "the third day He (I) shall rise again." This is the third time within a short span of time that Jesus foretold the passion (compare 16:21-22; 17:22-23).

20 Then came to him the mother of Zebedee's children with her sons, worshipping him, and desiring a certain thing of him. 21 And he said unto her, What wilt thou? She saith unto him, Grant that these my two sons may sit, the one on thy right hand, and the other on thy left, in thy kingdom.
Immediately following the prediction, James and John, the sons of Zebedee, came with their mother to ask for preferential treatment, i.e., that they both be given the privilege to sit on either side of Jesus in his kingdom. In Mark's account (10:35), James and John approached Jesus themselves, but here it was through their mother. Some scholars doubt the plausibility of this account historically, because in v. 22 of Matthew, Jesus directed His response to her sons only. However, the main point is not who came or who did not come, but that they did come. The fact is that the three were involved in the plot, and their mother was the spokesperson. Jesus responded appropriately, directly to the two disciples, because they should have known better. Their approach to Jesus with such a request, whether with their mother or not, showed that:

(1) they never understood Christ's teaching about humility (Matthew 18:1-4); (2) they were insensitive to the upcoming "painful" event that awaited their Master in the immediate future; and (3) they were clouded by their selfish ambitions. This affirmed what is known about their aggressiveness (Mark 9:38; Luke 9:54).

The three came before Jesus "worshipping him" (Greek *proskuvousa,*), i.e., to go on one's knees, to kneel before someone, to prostrate oneself in homage. This is a sign of reverence to a king and is consistent with African tradition. In Africa, especially among the Yorubas of Nigeria, one kneels down when speaking before one's superiors—the elders, traditional kings, and chiefs. Kneeling in the Bible expresses homage and worship to God (1 Kings 8:54; Ezra 9:5; Isaiah 45:23), and to Christ (Matthew 17:14; Mark 1:40; 10:17; Luke 5:8). Daniel 6:10 shows that kneeling in prayer was already a customary practice and shows humility before God in urgency of our request and petition. Kneeling down before someone shows desperation (Matthew 18:26, 29) and calls attention to the person making the petition.

When my children desperately need some help or something from their mother, or me, they go on their knees even before they speak. Immediately we see, and we ask them, "What do you want?" We have the same picture here. Apart from the fact that James and John, with their mother, may have prostrated themselves before Christ as a sign of homage in recognition of his Lordship, it was calling Jesus' attention to something important to them. Jesus was aware of this, hence He asked her, "What wilt thou?" In other words, "What is it that you want?" (NIV).

Her request was clear. She wanted her children to be given special places in the kingdom. To be on the "right hand" and the "left hand" of Christ in His kingdom meant having the highest position. It was a position of power and prestige, and they wanted to be part of that. This request may have been prompted by their cognizance of Jesus as the Messiah, and their going to Jerusalem. They expected the Messianic Glory to be revealed there. They, therefore, wanted to be sure of a prominent place in this kingdom. "Thy kingdom" (i.e., Christ's Kingdom) is the same as the "kingdom of heaven" (18:1-4) where Christ reigns in glory.

This shall be consummated at the Second Coming (Greek *Perousia*) of Christ. They probably thought that it was something near at hand without the suffering. This request further shows, like Peter (16:22), their ignorance in understanding the mission and purpose of Christ on earth. They (and the other disciples) could not fully comprehend the whole concept of Christ's suffering and death, even when they had been constantly taught and reminded, even after Jesus had just reminded them a second time (20:18-19)

22 But, Jesus answered and said, Ye know not what ye ask. Are ye able to drink of the cup that I shall drink of, and to be baptized with the baptism that I am baptized with? They said unto him, We are able.

Their ignorance is evidenced in Jesus' answer and subsequent question to them, "Ye know not what ye ask." Here Jesus turned to the brothers and firmly told them that they did not know what they were asking. They did not understand the implication of their request and what it took to reign with Christ (Matthew 10:37-39; Romans 8:17; 2 Timothy 2:12; Revelation 3:21). Jesus asked two direct questions, which have the same interpretation, regarding the suffering and death He would undergo. The "cup" (compare Matthew 26:39, 42; Mark 10:38; John 18:11) is the cup of suffering, an Old Testament image referring to punishment and retribution. Jesus asked them, "Are ye able to drink of the cup that I shall drink of, and to be baptized with the baptism that I am baptized with?" Their answer of affirmation continues to expose either their ignorance to the true nature of their request or reveals clearly how deeply their ambition for prominence was rooted in their minds.

This is very common today among the so-called Christian community. People are willing to do anything, to go through anything in quest for honor and worldly position. The "baptism" with which Christ was baptized also referred to the type of suffering Jesus was to undergo, imminently.

23 And he said unto them, Ye shall drink indeed of my cup, and be baptized with the same baptism that I am baptized with: but to sit on my right hand, and on my left, is not mine to give, but it shall be given to them for whom it is prepared of my Father.
Jesus' rebuttal to their bold answer is significant. Yes, Jesus seems to say, "You will indeed (surely) drink of my cup, and be baptized with the same baptism that I am baptized with." Jesus was predicting the suffering of the disciples, including the two brothers. Acts of the Apostles (12:2) recorded the death of James as the first Christian and apostolic martyr; and John suffered persecution and exile on the isolated island of Patmos (Revelation 1:9). However, it is not the role of Jesus to determine those who would sit by His side. That special privilege has been reserved for the Father. Jesus, in many places in the Bible, makes clear that there are certain rights which are the Father's (Mark 13:32; Acts 1:7) and that His authority is derived from the Father (Matthew 11:27; 24:36; 28:18; John 14:28).

What did Jesus mean by "It shall be given to them for whom it is prepared of my Father?" Who are those people to whom the kingdom has been prepared for? Does it mean that James and John are excluded?

24 And when the ten heard it, they were moved with indignation against the two brethren. 25 But Jesus called them unto him, and said, Ye know that the princes of the Gentiles exercise dominion over them, and they that are great exercise authority upon them.
When the other 10 disciples heard the request of James and John, they resented them—"they were moved with indignation against the brethren." "Indignation" is a translation of the Greek

aganakteo, compounded from "agan" (much) and *achthos* (grief). It means, "to be greatly afflicted, be much (sore) displeased." The disciples were greatly grieved in spirit because of the request, and it ignited much anger and hatred against the two brothers. Why were they so angry with them? Doubtless, their indignation sprang from their own selfishness and jealousy, the fear that they might lose out. It seems that they also desired the same position, but were not bold enough, as James and John, to come openly to Jesus to make the same request. They probably revert to the feud of an earlier period (Mark 9:33-37; compare Matthew 18:1). Jesus then called them again to order and started teaching them once again about the kingdom. He drew a contrast between power and greatness among the human society, i.e., the Gentiles (*ta ethne*) and the power among those who were the heirs of the kingdom. The Gentile or "pagan" princes probably referred to the Romans whose empire was characterized by power and authority. He said the Gentile princes, i.e., those in power, "exercise dominion over" and they "exercise authority upon" their subjects. To "exercise dominion" (Greek *katakupieuein*) means to lord over, i.e., to control, subjugate. "Exercise authority (Greek *katexousiazo*), means to have full privilege over, with the same idea of control. Literally, both phrases are parallel and mean to "tyrannize and oppress." Jesus told them that was how the Gentile leadership operated. He was quick to warn them that such structure should not characterize His disciples (v. 26a).

26 But, it shall not be so among you: but whosoever will be great among you, let him be your minister; 27 And whosoever will be chief among you, let him be your servant

Jesus insisted that this type of greatness was not to be found among them. Rather, greatness among Jesus' disciples was based on service (v. 26). Anyone who wanted to be great must become the servant: *diakonos* (i.e., "servant") one who carries the command of another. *Diakonos* does not mean "deacon" or "minister" (KJV) in the sense of its usage in our contemporary churches, in which it has become a position of religious or political power and a badge of honor. It was a position of humble service, rather than the hierarchical position it has become. In case the disciples misunderstood the full meaning of this teaching, Jesus repeated it in v. 27 using a stronger Greek word *doulos*. It is usually translated "servant," but better rendered "slave" (1 Corinthians 9:19; 2 Corinthians 4:5; 1 Peter 2:16), to bring out the real spirit of servitude that it demands. *Doulos* means one who gives himself or herself wholly to the will and service of another. Both ministers and servants in v. 26-27, according to one writer, refer to the lowest secular and ecclesiastical office among Christians. In the Gentile world, humility is regarded as wickedness, rather than as a virtue. Who will ever imagine giving a slave leadership? That is what Jesus tried to convey here. To the ordinary man, humility and servitude do not blend with leadership. Jesus' teaching of ethics in leadership and power radically opposed the world's standard. It is revolutionary in nature and practice.

28 Even as the Son of man came not to be ministered unto, but to minister, and to give his life a ransom for many.
Explaining this new look in greatness and power further, Jesus cited Himself as the perfect example of service to others. He is the prime example of humility and servanthood (Philippians 2:3-11). Jesus telling them that His coming into the world was not to be ministered to, i.e., not to lord it over others as the pagans do (Matthew 20:25), but rather to serve others (John 13:4-5). This verse gives the idea that Jesus, the Son of Man, because of His divine

origin, has every power, authority, and right with which to be served. Instead, He humbled Himself to the point of giving Himself as a sacrificial Lamb to atone for the sins of the world. Jesus spelled out His imminent passion and purpose of earthly advent, i.e., "to give his life as ransom for many." "Ransom," (Greek *lutron*) means redeeming, to pay a price for man, commonly used as a purchasing price to free slaves. The truth of Christ's teaching, exemplified by His humility, servitude, and redeeming death and His consequent exaltation to the kingdom, is clearly and dramatically presented by Paul in Philippians 2:3-11.

God exalted him to the highest place and gave the name that is above every name, that to the name of Jesus every knee should bow, in heaven and on earth and under the earth, and every tongue confess that Jesus Christ is Lord to the glory of God the Father. (Philippians 2:9-11, NIV)

The lesson James, John, their mother, and the rest of the disciples should have learned was that entrance into the kingdom required humility and a servant's spirit, unselfish ambition, and a desire to serve even to the point of suffering. "Whoever exalts himself will be humbled, and whoever humbles himself will be exalted" (Matthew 23:12; Luke 14:11; James 4:6, 10). Someone says that the way to greatness in the world is to go up by every means, even at the expense of others. The way of the gospel is to go down and become the least, a servant of all, considering others first (Philippians 2:3-4; Romans 12:16).

Forgiveness
Based on Matthew 18:21-35

DEFINING THE ISSUE

Son: "Daddy, why does Jesus talk so much about forgiveness?"

Father: "I think because it's something we all need to give and receive."

Forgiveness is an act of the will which releases another from the obligation to repay, restore, or reconcile a wrong they have committed against us or a debt they owe to us. Forgiveness is the ability to acknowledge the offense, but refuse to allow it to be a barrier between you and the person who has done you wrong. Forgiveness is a divine attribute that God shares with people everywhere. Healing energies are released when forgiveness is accepted and passed on.

In this study, Jesus illustrates the principle of forgiveness by using money as the focus. But the principle can also be applied to misunderstandings, harsh words, or physical abuse. The ability to forgive is a quality of God's personality that He put into our personalities. As God forgives, so can we.

AIM

By the end of the lesson, students will be able to accurately retell the parable of the unforgiving servant, have a deeper understanding of the meaning of forgiveness, and recognize the importance of accepting God's forgiveness and extending forgiveness to others.

SCRIPTURE TEXT

MATTHEW 18:21 Then came Peter to him, and said, Lord, how oft shall my brother sin against me, and I forgive him? till seven times?

22 Jesus saith unto him, I say not unto thee, Until seven times: but, Until seventy times seven.

23 Therefore is the kingdom of heaven likened unto a certain king, which would take account of his servants.

24 And when he had begun to reckon, one was brought unto him, which owed him ten thousand talents.

25 But forasmuch as he had not to pay, his lord commanded him to be sold, and his wife, and children, and all that he had, and payment to be made.

26 The servant therefore fell down, and worshipped him, saying, Lord, have patience with me, and I will pay thee all.

27 Then the lord of that servant was moved with compassion, and loosed him, and forgave him the debt.

28 But the same servant went out, and found one of his fellow-servants, which owed him an hundred pence: and he laid hands on him, and took him by the throat, saying, Pay me that thou owest.

29 And his fellow-servant fell down at his feet, and besought him, saying, Have patience with me, and I will pay thee all.

30 And he would not: but went and cast him into prison, till he should pay the debt.

31 So when his fellow-servants saw what was done, they were very sorry, and came and told unto their lord all that was done.

32 Then his lord, after that he had called him, said unto him, O thou wicked servant, I forgave thee all that debt, because thou desiredst me:

33 Shouldest not thou also have had compassion on thy fellow-servant, even as I had pity on thee?

34 And his lord was wroth, and delivered him to the tormentors, till he should pay all that was due unto him.

35 So likewise shall my heavenly Father do also unto you, if ye from your hearts forgive not every one his brother their trespasses.

BIBLE BACKGROUND

In the middle of Jesus' fourth discourse to the disciples and the multitudes, He began talking about people's relationships with one another (Matthew 18:15). He presented the procedure that Christians should follow to work out disputes among themselves. If a problem couldn't be resolved between two Christians, they should have one or two other Christians listen to the problem. If the problem was still not resolved, one must then bring it to the church. If the other Christian still refused to follow the church's resolutions, then he should be treated as one who didn't know God. Jesus concluded this teaching on relationships between Christians by reminding them that if two or three come together and pray in His name, their prayer will be answered (Matthew 18:20).

POINTS TO PONDER

1. *Jesus said that we are to forgive our brothers and sisters at least ____ times. (Matthew 18:22)*
2. *Servant number one (or Mr. Big Spender) owed the king 10,000 talents or about ____ million dollars. (v. 24)*
3. *Servant number two (or Mr. Few Dollars) owed his colleague 100 pence or about ____ dollars. (v. 28)*
4. *Servant number one was forgiven much, but because he refused to forgive his colleague a little, his ____ was retracted. (vv. 32-34)*
5. *God does not forgive us only ____ times (v. 22), but continually. However, we can only experience His forgiveness as we ____ others. (v. 35)*

LESSON AT-A-GLANCE

1. *The setting (Matthew 18:21-22)*
2. *The story (vv. 23-34)*
3. *The sense (v. 35)*

EXPLORING THE MEANING

1. The setting (Matthew 18:21-22)

Although Jesus chose 12 disciples to be with Him, to become prepared for ministry, and to eventually be sent out to help change the world, only a few of them are quoted in the New Testament. The most prominent disciple is Peter. He was Jesus' "first administrative assistant" and unofficial spokesperson for the disciples.

In the four listings of the disciples, Peter's name is always first (Matthew 10:2-4; Mark 3:16; Luke 6:14-16; Acts 1:13). So it is not surprising that he asked Jesus the question that provides the setting for today's parable. And we can suppose that he was asking for at least some of the other disciples as well. They had probably already discussed the "forgiveness question" and decided that forgiving somebody seven times was actually *more* than could be expected.

Dr. William Barclay, in his commentary on Matthew, informs us that the "official number of forgivenesses among the rabbis was three times" (*The Gospel of Matthew*, Vol. 2, Philadelphia: Westminster, 1975, p. 193). The disciples had already learned that Jesus usually required more of them than the rabbis. So they doubled the official figure, added one more time and arrived at seven as a good maximum number. Peter presented the question to Jesus, probably expecting Jesus' total agreement and a compliment for his wisdom.

Peter's question was, "Lord, if my brother keeps on sinning against me, how many times do I have to forgive him?" And then before Jesus could answer, he presented the number he and the disciples had probably discussed and agreed on. "Seven times?" (v. 21, TEV).

To their utter amazement, Jesus said, "No!" The disciples probably felt puzzled and relieved. Had they overestimated? Maybe Jesus agreed with the rabbis. Or maybe four, five, or six times was enough to forgive. Then Jesus put their minds at ease or at greater unease. He said that seven times was not enough times to forgive. In the kingdom of God, you must forgive others 70 times seven or 490 times.

Judas was the treasurer, and Matthew had been a tax collector, so they quickly figured out what Jesus was saying. According to

Jesus' principle of forgiveness, if a brother from the 'hood stole something out of your house every week for a year, four months, and five days, you were supposed to forgive him each time. If the "brother" stole your radio, CD or video player, television set, and whatever else he could get his hands on, and you caught him with the goods, and he said, "Man, like I'm sorry, please forgive me"— as a disciple, a Christian, a follower of Christ, the disciples and we, as believers, are supposed to forgive the brother (or sister)!

Can you see the disciples standing there? Amazed. Speechless. Flabbergasted! Looking at Jesus with blown minds and open mouths?

2. The story (vv. 23-34)
Jesus saw their dismay and said, "Let me tell you a story. It will show you how the principle of forgiveness operates in the kingdom of heaven that I've talked to you about before" (v. 23, paraphrased). Jesus said, "Once there was a king who decided to make an audit of his accounts receivables. His bookkeeper discovered that the king had loaned 'Mr. Big Spender' 10,000 talents or about 10 million dollars" (v. 24, LB). "The king told the bookkeeper to send the man a statement telling him to come in and bring this account up-to-date or prepare to go to jail. And the king instructed, 'Tell him if he can't pay, he must bring in a list of everything he owns, along with his wife and children, because they are going to jail too'" (v. 25, paraphrased).

Mr. Big Spender followed the king's instructions and appeared before the king with his account books and his wife and children. But just before the king could tell the guards to take him away, the man fell down on his hands and knees and said, "Please Mr. King. Please, I'm going to pay you, I just need some more time.

Please," he sobbed, "my wife…my kids…please give me some more time…some more time."

The king's security guards had witnessed scenes like this before, so they just moved in to put the cuffs on Mr. Big Spender. But he kept crying, "Please, Mr. King…just a little more time…my wife…my kids…just a little more time!"

The king looked at him and was "moved with compassion" (v. 27). He felt "a sympathetic consciousness of [Mr. Big Spender's] distress" (*Webster's Dictionary*). As he sat there watching, did he remember times before he became king—times when he owed lots of money? Times when he had been on the edge of bankruptcy, poverty, and prison? Did he think of his own wife and children? "Let him go," the king told the security guards. "Yes, let him go." Then he looked at Mr. Big Spender and said, "Take your wife and kids and go home. You don't owe me anything. Your debt is forgiven" (v. 27, paraphrased).

Jesus was an excellent storyteller and, by this time, no doubt the disciples were almost in tears. Jesus paused to let the first part of the story sink in. He took a deep breath and said, "BUT," paused again and went on.

But that same man went out and saw one of his colleagues, Mr. Few Dollars, who "owed him an hundred pence" (or about $2,000.00 (v. 28, LB). The next thing Mr. Few Dollars knew, Mr. Big Spender had him by the throat and was screaming, "Pay me my money. Pay me my so-and-so money!" Somehow Mr. Few Dollars managed to get down on his knees with Mr. Big Spender still choking him. He managed to gasp out, "Please, Bro', I'm going to pay you, but I need a little more time. I don't get paid 'til Friday. Man, can't you wait until Friday?"

Big Spender said, "No, I've waited long enough, you're gonna do some time. Hey!" he said to the police. "Throw this man in jail 'til he pays me my money!" The police dragged Mr. Few Dollars away, still hollering, "Man, I'm going to pay you Friday. Can't you wait 'til Friday?"

Some of Mr. Big Spender's friends just happened to be passing by, saw what happened and said, "Wow…man…wasn't that Big Spender choking Few Dollars? The same Big Spender the king just got through forgiving of a 10-million-dollar debt?"

Jesus paused again and looked at the disciples with a "can-you-believe-it!" expression. They all looked back at Jesus with a "what-happened-next?" expression on their faces.

Jesus said that Mr. King called Mr. Big Spender back in, gave him an unforgettable tongue lashing, called him "wicked" (v. 32), and had Mr. Big Spender thrown in jail for a long, long time.

Jesus then added, "That is how my Father in heaven will treat every one of you [maybe He paused and looked each one of them in the eye] unless you forgive your brother from your heart" (v. 35, TEV).

3. The sense (v. 35)

There are at least two important lessons in Jesus' parable:

Lesson one: *We should not borrow beyond our ability to pay.*

Mr. Big Spender and Mr. Few Dollars owed different amounts of money, but they both had the same problem: they borrowed more than they could pay back. There are persons who interpret the Apostle Paul's phrase, "Owe no man anything" (Romans 13:8, KJV) to mean that Christians should be completely debt-free. There are other Christians who interpret the phrase in its context and believe that some financial debt is permitted. Being debt-free does have its advantages, perhaps in terms of providing peace of mind and greater flexibility or mobility in the use of one's time, and the reinvestment and deployment of one's financial resources.

However, in the purchase of expensive items such as a home, car, or an educational investment, sometimes borrowing money is the only way, or the most efficient way, to achieve one's purpose. However, a Christian (or anyone else) should never borrow and agree to pay back $1,000.00 a month, for example, when receiving only $800.00 a month of spendable income. To avoid the predicament of the debtors in our story, one must balance the accumulation of debt with the ability to pay.

Lesson two: *We should ask for forgiveness only if we are willing to forgive.*

This is the central lesson of this parable, isn't it?

God's forgiveness is unlimited. The *quality* of God's forgiveness is not determined by the *quantity* of our sins. Notice the numbers in the parable. God will not only forgive us 490 times (v. 22), but millions of times (v. 24). God's forgiveness is unlimited. But our *experience* of forgiveness is dependent on our giving of forgiveness.

This is not as simple as it sounds at first, because forgiveness is an automatic reflex with God! That is, God forgives us not because we beg Him or even ask Him. God forgives us because of who He is. God forgives us because He *is* love (1 John 4:8). The emphasis here is that God not only shows love, provides, and gives love; God *is* love. And the nature of love is to forgive. So when we sin, God does not hold the sin against us, waiting to see if we're going to ask Him or beg Him for forgiveness. No, just as love is ever-flowing from God's nature to us, so forgiveness is ever-flowing from Him and always available to us.

The "forgiveness problem" is not God's but ours. God's forgiveness is always available, but we can only receive forgiveness when we meet the conditions. In a sense, it's like a high school education. In our country, a high school education is available to all citizens of high school age and older. But a high school education is received only by those who fulfill the requirements.

God's forgiveness is available to all, but those who experience forgiveness are those who *ask for it, accept it*, and pass it on to others. Mr. Big Spender asked for it, and received it, but did not experience it because he was not willing to pass it on to Mr. Few Dollars.

All of us have sinned (Romans 3:23), but it is so exciting and reassuring to know that we can experience God's forgiveness, no matter what the quality or quantity of our sins, IF we are willing to ask for forgiveness, accept it, and pass it on.

DISCERNING MY DUTY

1. *Is it possible to have God's forgiveness available to us and not be able to experience His forgiveness? If so, how is such a situation possible?*
2. *Should we keep a count of the number of times we forgive people? What kind of effect might keeping count have on the quality of our forgiveness?*
3. *Does God keep count of the number of times He forgives us? (See Jeremiah 31:33-34.)*
4. *Should we refuse to forgive a person, if we know that person has not forgiven someone else?*
5. *Should we endeavor to pay our debts, or just ask the people we owe to forgive the debt? (See Matthew 6:12.)*

DECIDING MY RESPONSE

1. *Should Christian churches borrow money from secular institutions such as banks, credit unions, and insurance companies to finance their building and expansion programs?*

2. *What might be the results if African American churches pooled their resources and bought hotels, restaurants, and other public facilities to use for their annual meetings, conferences, and conventions?*
3. *Is it right for nations to forgive each other? Should the United States forgive Japan for its attack on Pearl Harbor? Should Israel forgive Germany for the murder of six million Jews? Should African Americans forgive white Americans and Europeans for enslaving us?*
4. *Take some special time alone and search your mind and heart to discover anyone that you haven't forgiven. If the Lord brings anyone to your mind, ask Him to forgive you for not having already forgiven this person. Then ask the Lord for special grace and strength to forgive the person or persons completely and without reservation.*
5. *If you owe anybody money, go pay them or make proper arrangements.*
6. *If you are not a tither, begin paying your tithes. According to Malachi 3:8-10, we owe God one-tenth of what He blesses us to earn. Right?*

LIGHT ON THE HEAVY

Forgiveness. Hebrew and Greek, the original Bible languages, have several words that translate into English as "forgive." Some of the Hebrew words mean to pardon, to cover, to let pass, take away, wash, hide, and purify. Some of the Greek words mean to send away, leave, omit, and to let go. It is noteworthy that divine forgiveness is distinctively a biblical concept. The idea is present in Islam, but not as prominent as in Judaism and Christianity. It is in the Bible that forgiveness comes to its own and has remained an important feature of the Hebrew-Christian tradition. (Adapted from P.H. Monsama, "Forgiveness" *Zondervan's Pictorial Encyclopedia of the Bible*, Vol. 2, 1976, p. 596).

MORE LIGHT ON THE TEXT

Jesus has just finished teaching the disciples how to deal with disputes in the church, where one brother has offended another. First, the one who has caused the offense is directly approached by the one offended for settlement. If that does not work, the church is to become involved. If the brother refuses to change, then he should be disciplined (v. 15-17). In verses 18-20, Jesus speaks of the power that the church has, because of His permanent presence in the church.

Matthew 18:21 Then came Peter to him, and said, Lord, how oft shall my brother sin against me, and I forgive him? Till seven times? 22 Jesus saith unto him, I say not unto thee, Until seven times: but, Until seventy times seven.

Matthew introduces the next sequence of events with the conjunction "then," (*tote*), and links the preceding event with the ones that follow. *Tote* is used to introduce that which follows in time, and, therefore, can be rendered: "at that time," or "after that," and so on. Perhaps, prompted by the teaching of forgiveness, Peter approached Jesus and asked a follow-up question about forgiveness, using a practical example. The issue was not referring to the decision of the church, but personal forgiveness (compare Matthew 6:14-15; Mark 11:25; Luke 17:3-4). "How oft shall my brother sin against me, and I forgive him?" Peter asked and interjected, "Till seven times?" In the rabbinical community, the agreement was that a brother might be forgiven for a repeated sin three times, after that, there was no forgiveness.

Why did Peter come up with seven? Was he trying to be magnanimous by suggesting "seven times?" Alternatively, was he following a common thread of the use of seven in the Bible? It is generally suggested that the number seven indicates completeness, using the Genesis creation account as the basis (Genesis 2:1-3; compare Leviticus 4:6; 26:21; Numbers 19:4; Joshua 6:4; Proverbs 24:16). The Greek phrase translated "my brother" is *adelphos* and could be a blood-related sibling or anyone of the same religious society, as in verse 15.

Jesus' reply, "I say not unto thee," suggested that this situation had been discussed earlier, and perhaps Peter did not understand it clearly. Jesus then said not "seven times," but "until seventy times seven." In Luke 17:3b-4, Jesus said, "If your brother sins… against you seven times in a day, and seven times comes back to you and says, 'I repent,' forgive him." What does Jesus mean by 70 times 7? Reading it with a Greek or English understanding, it equals 70x7 (490), but with the Roman numerals LXX, which has a rendering of the Hebrew understanding, it means 70+7 (77). Jesus alluded to Genesis 4:24, transforming Lamech's revenge into a principle for forgiveness. In this context, Jesus is not setting 490 or 77 times as the upper limit for forgiveness, but teaches that frequency or quantity should not qualify regarding forgiveness. The parable that follows vividly illustrates the extent, rather than the frequency, of forgiveness. It further shows that we are forgiven far more than we can ever forgive.

23 Therefore is the kingdom of heaven likened unto a certain king, which would take account of his servants.
Jesus illustrated His point with a parable. "Therefore," since Jesus required His disciples to forgive those who offended them, the kingdom of heaven could be compared with a king who removed

the record of his debtors. "The kingdom of heaven" means the sovereignty of God over the universe and is paralleled with the kingdom of God. The kingdom of heaven is personified by God, who was represented in the parable by an earthly king. Those in the kingdom are the servants (*douloi*, literally slaves) serving a great king. The servants may include high-ranking officials in a huge colonial empire, since the amount of money was a huge sum (v. 24). The king decides to take account (Greek *sunairo* literally means to compare accounts). (Compare with Matthew 25:19.)

24 And when he had begun to reckon, one was brought unto him, which owed him ten thousand talents. 25 But forasmuch as he had not to pay, his lord commanded him to be sold, and his wife, and children, and all that he had, and payment to be made. 26 The servant therefore fell down, and worshipped him, saying, Lord, have patience with me, and I will pay thee all.

One of the officials who owed 10,000 talents was brought to the attention of the king. Some people have estimated the dollar value of one talent (Greek *talanton*) of gold to be about $29,085.00, and 10,000 would be $290,085,000. A talent of silver is estimated at $1,920.00 and 10,000 would be $19,920,000 (*Dake's Annotated Reference Bible*, see note at Matthew 18:24). An idea of the size of the debt can be compared with the donation for the construction of the temple where David gave 3,000 talents of gold and 7,000 talents of silver. The princes donated 5,000 talents of gold and 10,000 talents of silver (1 Chronicles 29:4, 7). In today's currency value, with the fluctuating price of precious metals coupled with inflation, these figures would run into billions or trillions of dollars. However, the amount was used to compare the extent of the forgiveness and mercy shown to the servant-debtor and the amount owed to him by his fellow servant (v. 28) for whom he showed no mercy.

The servant appeared before the king and was not able to pay the king what he owed. The king ordered that he and his family (his wife and children), with all their possessions, be sold into slavery in order to recover the debt. The practice of being sold for a debt is consistent with the practice in the Old Testament (Leviticus 25:39; 2 Kings 4:1). It is the most severe and humiliating punishment for anyone to endure. The aim of selling the entire family was not to recover the full amount owed, but to punish. If top price for a slave would fetch one talent or less, as some suggest, then the total price of the family would not be enough to cover the debt. This was a punishment and such slaves, therefore, must be freed in the year of jubilee, every 50 years (see Leviticus 25:10, 28). The servant, desperate and hopeless, fell down on his knees and pled for time, "Be patient with me, I will pay back everything," he said. The phrase "fell down, and worshipped him" (Greek *prosekunei*) is the imperfect tense of the Greek verb *prosekuneo*, which is to go on one's knees, to kneel before someone, or to prostrate oneself in homage (Matthew 20:20). The servant falling down and worshiping him, served a dual purpose: paying homage was a sign of a desperate plea to his lord (master). This honor was reserved for kings and people of higher positions in the society.

27 Then the lord of that servant was moved with compassion, and loosed him, and forgave him the debt.
Seeing his desperation, helplessness, and his inability to pay such a huge amount, his lord was moved with compassion and forgave him the whole amount he owed. To be "moved with compassion" in (Greek *splagchnistheis*) is to have sympathy or to pity. The lord was moved with pity and he forgave him the "debt" (Greek

daneion), which is better translated "loan." The lord treated the debt as a bad loan and wrote it off. The servant didn't have to pay it back. He was totally freed from any obligation. The phrase, "loosed him" (in Greek *luo*), is to untie and suggests that he was arrested and bound before they brought him before the king, and had now been completely released (set free) when the lord forgave him. In this case, the debt was treated, at first, as embezzlement, but now the king canceled it, as a bad loan, and forgave the servant.

28 But the same servant went out, and found one of his fellow-servants, which owed him an hundred pence: and he laid his hands on him, and took him by the throat, saying, Pay me that thou owest. 29 And his fellow-servant fell down at his feet, and besought him, saying, Have patience with me, and I will pay thee all. 30 And he would not: but went and cast him into prison, till he should pay the debt.

Verses 28-30 give a complete opposite picture of verses 24-27. The servant who received mercy from his master for the huge amount of "money" owed, showed no mercy to his fellow servant who owed a few talents. Jesus linked the preceding story with the conjunction, "but," which immediately struck a note of contrast with and introduced the next phase of the parable. Having been forgiven his debt, the servant probably rushed out of the king's court with celebration of joy. He found another servant, lower in rank than he, in the outer courtyard, who owed him 100 "pence" (i.e., 100 *denarii*, NIV). According to Dake's Annotated Reference Bible, one penny is equivalent to $0.17; 100 pence is $17.00. The amount might be high in their standard, but very insignificant compared with the amount forgiven him. Immediately, he mercilessly grabbed the servant by the throat choking him and demanded that the debt be paid immediately. His fellow servant pleaded with him to be patient with him, that he would eventually pay him everything he owed. The similarity of the plea (v. 29) to his own plea to the king (v. 26) did not move this unforgiving man. Rather than showing mercy, he had him thrown into a debtor's prison and ordered that he be remanded there until he paid the amount in full.

31 So when his fellow-servants saw what was done, they were very sorry, and came and told unto their lord all that was done. The other servants, who witnessed what had happened, were distressed because of such cruelty, and went out to report to the master. The phrase "they were very sorry" is the Greek phrase *elupethesan sphodra*, which means "greatly grieved." They were not merely sorry, but were severely touched in the heart to the point of grieving. They were not merely sympathetic, they empathized with the fellow servant, and showed it by reporting it to their master. The word rendered "told" *diesaphesan* from *dia-saphew* is a strong verb, which means to explain, or to narrate, used only twice in the New Testament, here and in Matthew 13:36 as the word declared. They explained in detail what the unforgiving servant had done.

32 Then his lord, after that he had called him, said unto him, O thou wicked servant, I forgave thee all that debt, because thou desirest me: 33 Shouldest not thou also have had compassion on thy fellow-servant, even as I had pity on thee? 34 And his lord was wroth, and delivered him to the tormentors, till he should pay all that was due unto him.
On hearing this report, the master called in the unforgiving servant, and reprimanded him, denouncing him for what he had done and

called him a "wicked servant." He asked him why he could not forgive his fellow servant as he was forgiven. Of course, he had no answer, and the master expected no answer. There was no amount of explanation that would exonerate him for his wicked action. The master was so upset that, instead of selling him (v. 25), he turned him over to the tormentors. In the Greek language *basanisteis* means torturers, not merely "jailers" (NIV). The word refers to jailers who have charge of the prisoners and who torture them when asked to do so. The servant was to be tortured in prison until he paid back all that he owed, which was impossible.

35 So likewise shall my heavenly Father do also unto you, if ye from your hearts forgive not every one his brother their trespasses.

Jesus concluded the parable by comparing the reaction of the master to the unmerciful servant with what God would do to those who did not forgive others their trespasses. This parable demonstrates the necessity of forgiveness and how we should treat one another. Jesus advocates that we forgive from our "hearts" those who have wronged us. "From the heart" here means genuine and sincere forgiveness. Concluding His teaching on prayer, Jesus told His disciples that they ought to forgive others as they have been forgiven, lest our "Father will not forgive [your] sins" (Matthew 6:12, 14-15).

This parable does not deal with frequency, but illustrates the extent of forgiveness we have received from our heavenly Father through the death of His Son. We are forgiven far more than we can ever forgive. Certain questions arise from this parable. When do we forgive our brothers: before or after they have confessed? Do we have to forgive whether they repent or not? What does it mean to love your enemies and do good to those who hate you? As Christians, we have been forgiven much, and we should forgive much.

The Gospel Has No Boundaries
Based on Acts 17:22-34

DEFINING THE ISSUE

Deborah entered the fabulous Sheraton Hotel in New Orleans, not really knowing why she was there. Two days earlier, as she was planning to rest quietly at home, she believed she was prompted by the Holy Spirit to make an arrangement to attend a church convention in New Orleans. Deborah obeyed and went to New Orleans.

Deborah walked around the hotel, observing the delegates as they arrived and went to their assigned rooms. She observed a young lady sitting in the lounge reading her Bible. Deborah went and sat next to her, greeted her, and soon entered into a discussion on how to know God personally. The young lady was curious and receptive to all that Deborah shared about God's love, Christ's life, His death, His resurrection, and how she could know God through Jesus Christ. When Deborah finished showing the young lady various verses in the Bible, she asked her if she would like to know God through praying and asking Christ to come into her life as Saviour and Lord. The young lady said, "Yes," and the angels in heaven rejoiced as another soul was saved.

Deborah hadn't planned to be in the Sheraton Hotel in New Orleans that weekend, but God had another plan for her. He had a special job for her to do. Similarly, Paul had not intended to preach in Athens during this time, but God had other plans. Today's lesson will teach us more about God's plans for Paul in Athens.

AIM

By the end of the lesson, the students will be able to summarize the Gospel message preached by Paul, will become more convinced of the significance of the Gospel as truth, and commit themselves to share it with others.

SCRIPTURE TEXT

ACTS 17:22 Then Paul stood in the midst of Mars' hill, and said, Ye men of Athens, I perceive that in all things ye are too superstitious.

23 For as I passed by, and beheld your devotions, I found an altar with this inscription, TO THE UNKNOWN GOD. Whom therefore ye ignorantly worship, him declare I unto you.

24 God that made the world and all things therein, seeing that he is Lord of heaven and earth, dwelleth not in temples made with hands;

25 Neither is worshipped with men's hands, as though he needed anything, seeing he giveth to all life, and breath, and all things;

26 And hath made of one blood all nations of men for to dwell on all the face of the earth, and hath determined the times before appointed, and the bounds of their habitation;

27 That they should seek the Lord, if haply they might feel after him, and find him, though he be not far from every one of us:

28 For in him we live, and move, and have our being; as certain also of your own poets have said, For we are also his offspring.

29 Forasmuch then as we are the offspring of God, we ought not to think that the Godhead is like unto gold, or silver, or stone, graven by art and man's device.

30 And the times of this ignorance God winked at; but now commandeth all men everywhere to repent:

31 Because he hath appointed a day, in the which he will judge the world in righteousness by that man whom he hath ordained; whereof he hath given assurance unto all men, in that he hath raised him from the dead.

32 And when they heard of the resurrection of the dead, some mocked: and others said, We will hear thee again of this matter.

33 So Paul departed from among them.

34 Howbeit certain men clave unto him, and believed: among the which was Dionysius the Areopagite, and a woman named Damaris, and others with them.

BIBLE BACKGROUND

Paul's preaching in Athens, at this time, was not planned by him, but planned by God. Apparently, he was on his way to Macedonia when providential actions prevented him, for God was protecting him from persecution in Macedonia. Paul was waiting for Silas and Timothy to come before beginning his mission in Athens. But, as he observed the rampant idolatry in Athens, he was compelled to present the claims of Christ to the Jews and "God-fearing" Gentiles. Paul preached in the synagogue on the Sabbath and to whomever would listen in the marketplace on weekdays. It was during this time of preaching that some Athenians led Paul to the Areopagus (Mars' Hill) where the Council met. They wanted Paul to share more of this "new teaching" (vv. 18-20). Paul did share, but did they comprehend and accept the Gospel for all mankind? Today's lesson will teach us what Paul shared on Mars' Hill and how the Athenians responded to the truth.

POINTS TO PONDER

Read Acts 17:22-34, then ponder the answers to the following questions.

1. *What did Paul observe in Athens that informed him of their ignorance about the true God? (v. 23)*

2. *Why is it that Paul could bluntly state that God does not live in temples built by human hands? (vv. 24-25)*

3. *Why did God make mankind to inhabit the whole earth? (vv. 26-27)*

4. What does God demand that all humankind do? (v. 30)

5. What caused the mixed response among the people who heard Paul's message? (v. 32)

LESSON AT-A-GLANCE

1. *The unknown God (Acts 17:22-23)*
2. *God the Creator (vv. 24-28)*
3. *God of all mankind (vv. 29-34)*

EXPLORING THE MEANING

1. The unknown God (Acts 17:22-23)

Paul, having observed that Athens was full of idols, could not keep silent, for the Word of God burned within him like a fire in his bones. He continually preached the Good News about Jesus to the Jews and the "God-fearing" Greeks in the synagogue and in the marketplace. Paul often had great discussions with the philosophers in Athens. On one occasion, the philosophers led Paul to a place called "Mars' Hill," or "Areopagus," to hear more about the Good News concerning Jesus. Areopagus literally means the "Court Council of Ares," and was the name for the Greek god of thunder and war. In the middle of this important place, filled with judges and city officials, Paul stood up to preach (17:22). He began by saying, "Ye men of Athens, I perceive that in all things ye are too superstitious" (v. 22). Paul was not being disrespectful by calling them "superstitious." He was stating that he observed them to be very religious and reverent for their gods.

Paul explained why he characterized them as very religious. He had walked around Athens and observed their devotions to the many objects of worship. They had temples, altars, statues, shrines, and other various sacrificial monuments in connection with their worship to these gods. Paul gave further explanation by stating specifically that he had observed an "altar with this inscription, TO THE UNKNOWN GOD. Whom therefore ye ignorantly worship" (v. 23). It is not surprising that Paul saw the inscription on that altar. Throughout history, the phrase "unknown God" was used in relation to the worship of the Athenians. In the second century, geographer Pausanias, and in the third century, philosopher Philostratus, spoke of altars to unknown gods in Athens. Nor was it surprising for Paul to have bluntly stated that they worship ignorantly, without knowing His name. But he gave them a solution, proclaiming to them the true, known God.

2. God the Creator (vv. 24-28)

Paul's desire was for his audience to know the true God. First, he described God as the One who "made the world and all things therein, seeing that he is Lord of heaven and earth, [and] dwelleth not in temples made with hands" (v. 24). This description contradicted his audience's opinion that there were many gods. Paul stated clearly that the true God created the world and everything in it. This also contradicted the belief that all things were controlled by fate. Second, he declared God as Lord of heaven and earth. This fact made it impossible for Him to live in temples made by humans. Third, Paul declared that the true God, "is not worshipped with men's hands, as though he needed anything, seeing he giveth to all life, and breath, and all things, nor is He made by men's hands" (v. 25). This contradicted those who believed that gods were fed or nourished by the offerings made to them. God, the Great Creator of all things, cannot be dependent on His creatures for anything. For He is the One who gives to all people life, breath, and everything else. Humans have nothing, but what we have, we receive from the hand of our Maker.

Yes, God also made people, for He "made of one blood all nations of men for to dwell on all the face of the earth, and hath determined the times before appointed, and the bounds of their habitation" (v. 26). God made of "one blood" refers to the creation of the first humans, Adam and Eve. From Adam, God made the nations of all people to live on the earth. This contradicted the Athenians' boast that they had originated from the soil of their Attic homeland, and, therefore, were not like other people. Paul desired to make it clear that everyone was made by God and was a descendant from a common ancestor. God has also appointed the time and place in which every person lives (v. 26b). He has wisely given to everyone their place to dwell.

God created all humankind in order that "they should seek the Lord, if haply they might feel after him, and find him, though he be not far from every one of us" (v. 27). God desires that every person from every nation should seek Him. He wants everyone to know of His existence and His character. God has made it possible for all nations, though living in different regions and climates, to have the opportunity to know God the Creator.

Although the opportunity to know God is available to all people, we have a responsibility. For this reason, Paul stated, "if haply they might feel after him, and find him" (v. 27). The phrase "if haply" implies that it is possible to find God. People cannot only find God, but "feel after him." This means that we can know and have a relationship with God even though He is transcendent and beyond our ability to completely understand Him. This is possible because "he is not far from every one of us" (v. 27b).

Paul emphasized God as the Creator by quoting two of the Athenian's own Greek poets (v. 28). The first quote, "For in him we live, and move, and have our being" was from the poet Epimenides. The words, "in him we live" implies that God originally formed us and continually sustains us. He is the original fountain of life and upholds us each moment. The phrase "and move" stresses that people need God for the ability to perform even the slightest motion. And the concept that we "have our being" emphasizes that if we live at all it is a gift from God. No words can better express our constant dependence on God.

The last phrase of verse 28, "for we are also his offspring," was a quote from the poet, Aratus. Aratus was a Greek poet of Cilicia and lived about 277 years before Christ. Paul was probably acquainted with Cilicia's writings. Paul used the above phrase to connect the theory portion of his message to the application part.

3. God of all mankind (vv. 29-34)

Paul reached the climax of his message by concluding that since "we are God's offspring" there must be a change in our thinking. As God's offspring, we are living and intelligent beings. So "we ought not to think that the Godhead is like unto gold, or silver, or stone, graven by art and man's devices" (v. 29). We should no longer think of God in terms of gold, silver, or stone made by human beings. It is absurd to suppose that the original source of our existence can be like these non-living objects.

In the past, God may have overlooked our ignorance when we thought of Him in this way, but now He demands people to change their way of thinking. Paul used the phrase, "but now commandeth all men everywhere to repent" (v. 30). God commands that all people, not just the Jews, repent and turn to Him. He had also set a time to judge all humankind by their acceptance of Jesus as Saviour. God proved that there will be a judgment day through the resurrection of Jesus Christ (v. 31). Not only did Jesus die for the sins of all people, He rose again; proof that there will be a judgment day when all people will be judged. The resurrection is absolute confirmation that Jesus is who He said He is, and that all people must accept Him personally or take responsibility for their rejection of Him.

The teaching of Jesus' resurrection brought immediate reaction from Paul's audience. Some mocked. Others said, "We will hear thee again of this matter" (v. 32). Some Greeks mocked because even though they had a belief in immortality, they denied any bodily resurrection. Jews that were present probably mocked because of their concept of immortality, even though they accepted the belief of resurrection. Others were more polite and suggested that they would like to hear more from Paul later.

Paul preached the full Gospel from his heart, beginning with God's love in creating people and their need to repent. The highlight of his speech was Jesus' death and resurrection. Unfortunately, he failed to convince most of the council at Mars' Hill of the truth of his message. "So Paul departed from among them" (v. 33). However, God's Word never returns void. Some followed Paul, believing in God the Creator and Jesus the Saviour. Two believers, Dionysius and Damaris, followed Paul. Dionysius also was a member of the council of Ares. Paul clearly explained to his audience that the Gospel is for all people, regardless of race, nationality, or sex. Human beings have the responsibility to accept or reject this Gospel.

DISCERNING MY DUTY

1. Give further explanation of what Paul meant by the phrase, "because he himself gives all men life and breath and everything else" (Acts 17:25).
2. If "God is not far from us" (v. 27), how do we go about finding him? Give specific actions we can take.
3. Based on verses 29-30, what should be our thinking about the nature and character of God?

DECIDING MY RESPONSE

Religious debates occur frequently in our society. They either arouse or turn off the hearers. Yet few Christians today could effectively debate why they believe God to be the one true God and only accessible through Jesus Christ. Of course, as Christians, we don't need to win debates about our faith, but we do need to know what we believe and why so we can help others understand these truths. This kind of preparation requires serious study of God's Word and, if possible, classes in basic Christian beliefs.

Read Acts 17:24-31 again. Then write down three facts about our relationship with God. For example, in verse 25, God is the one who gives all people the ability to have life. After writing these facts down, think of one person with whom you can share them this week. Then prayerfully ask God to prepare that person's heart to receive these truths. Look for an opportunity to ask the person at the end, if they know God intimately through having received Jesus Christ as their personal Saviour.

LIGHT ON THE HEAVY

Athenians. The Athenians were religious and eager to discuss religion. Their spiritual level and ability to comprehend spiritual truths, however, were not exceptionally high. They were noted for festivals to their gods and the love of human slaughter in the gladiatorial games.

Athens. Athens was famous for its culture, great dramatists, and philosophers like Plato and Aristotle. It was also famous for its temples, statues, and monuments.

Areopagus/Mars' Hill. A little hill in the northwest part of Athens, often called Mars' Hill in correspondence to the Roman Mars, where the council of the city met. It became known as the council of the Areopagus, because Areopagus was their original meeting place. (*New Bible Dictionary*, edited by I. Howard Marshall, A.R. Millard, J. I. Packer, D.J. Wiseman. Downers Grove: Inter-Varsity Press, 1996, 101-2, 79).

MORE LIGHT ON THE TEXT

In the verses which form the background to our text, Paul and Silas were forced to leave Thessalonica because some of the Jews there were uncomfortable with the success of Paul's preaching, for many were coming to the Lord (Acts 17:5-9). When Paul and Silas arrived at Berea, they began to preach and many people believed. Among them were some prominent Grecian women. The Jews at Thessalonica heard that many were converted at Berea and came to stir up the people against Paul and Silas. Paul was forced again to flee to Athens, leaving Silas and Timothy behind (vv. 10-15).

While waiting for Silas and Timothy to arrive from Berea, Paul spent time preaching and teaching in the synagogue, and reasoning daily with some of the Jews and some "God-fearing" Greeks. Then Paul was invited to Areopagus to meet with a group of philosophers called Epicureans and Stoics, who wanted to hear more of "this new teaching." "You are bringing some strange ideas to our ears, and we want to know about them," they said to Paul (v. 20).

Acts 17:22 Then Paul stood in the midst of Mars' hill, and said, Ye men of Athens, I perceive that in all things ye are too superstitious.

Having been given an open invitation into the Areopagus, Paul did not hesitate to preach the Good News about Jesus and His coming judgment. The people were ready to hear anything new, including what Paul had to say (v. 21). Paul then stood in the midst of the center of the court and began by commending the Athenians for their religiosity. He told them, "I perceive that in all things ye are superstitious." The word "superstitious" is the Greek word, *deisidaimon*, which means rendering reverence to gods, i.e., to be religious. The phrase can be reworded, thus, "I see that in every respect that you are devoutly religious people." This, however, has a negative connotation to it.

23 For as I passed by, and beheld your devotions, I found an altar with this inscription, TO THE UNKNOWN GOD. Whom therefore ye ignorantly worship, him declare I unto you.

Paul told them how he arrived at his conclusion. While walking along the streets of Athens, he had noticed that it was an idolatrous city (v. 16). He also saw, among all the other religious installations, an altar with the inscription "TO THE UNKNOWN GOD." This caught his attention. It showed how openly devoted the people were to religious worship. Paul used the inscription as a point of contact to introduce to them the Gospel about the "unknown God." While asserting that they did not know Him, Paul affirmed that the God whom they ignorantly (*agnoountes*) worship, was the same God the apostle was about to make known to them. Paul tried to emphasize their ignorance and the nonsense of their idol worship. They were so idolatrous that they worshipped even things that they did not know. Paul, in effect, said, "that which you worship and openly acknowledge in your ignorance, is what I am here to declare to you."

It was forbidden to preach about a new deity in Athens. Paul, therefore, simply used their own inscription to declare that the "Unknown God" was He whom Paul is representing. He was not bringing a new religion or introducing a new deity. Paul began by telling them about the true God, starting from the creation (what is known) to the biblical revelation and redemption (what is not known).

24 God that made the world and all things therein, seeing that he is Lord of heaven and earth, dwelleth not in temples made with hands; 25 Neither is worshipped with men's hands, as though he needed anything, seeing he giveth to all life, and breath, and all things.

Paul said that God, unknown to them, was the one who created the universe and everything in it. This God was the One who also created heaven, and he could not inhabit man-made sanctuaries. Paul's language is reminiscent of the Old Testament declaration of God's greatness. Solomon acknowledged the greatness of God when he declared, "But will God indeed dwell on the earth? behold, the heaven and the heaven of heavens cannot contain thee; how much less this house that I have builded?" (see 1 Kings 8:27; Isaiah 66:1). Indeed, Stephen also referred to both passages as he declared the greatness of God and confirmed that he did not dwell in temples made by man, not even in the temple erected for worship to Him in Jerusalem. Paul showed that God was unlike the numerous Athenian idols that were shut up in temples. These idols could not be the true God they wanted to worship. Paul was evidently attacking all the Greek idolatry, and how small their gods were, since they could fit into tiny spaces that were manmade. Paul also said that the true God, the Creator of all things, did not need anything from His creatures. He doesn't even need our worship. The phrase, "Neither is worshipped," (Greek *therapeutai* from *therapeuo*, meaning to wait upon, to minister, or to serve) demonstrates that. Note the difference between the Greek word used here for worship (*therapeuo*), and the one used in verse 23 (*eusebes*, from *eusebeo* meaning to be reverent, to respect, or to show piety towards someone). This term is usually used with respect to devotion toward the divine, i.e., spiritual worship. But here (v. 25), the idea of worship was giving material things as offerings of worship, which the Athenians were doing with the use of their images. This seems to be the practice in all religions. God does not need people to wait upon Him or serve Him by offering things, as if He needs anything from His creatures. Neither does His existence depend on human worship. Prophet Micah warns Israel against the notion that they can offer things to God to compensate for their disobedience (Micah 6:6-8). God declares through the psalmist:

I will take no bullock out of thy house, nor he goats out of thy folds. For every beast of the forest is mine, and the cattle upon a thousand hills. I know all the fowls of the mountains: and the wild beasts of the field are mine. If I were hungry, I would not tell thee: for the world is mine, and the fulness thereof. Will I eat the flesh of bulls, or drink the blood of goats? (Psalm 50:9-13).

Paul was indirectly attacking their images, the services, and the offerings they gave them. The Unknown God required none of these things. Rather, He was the One who supplied every need of theirs; He was the One who gave life, breath, and all things to all creatures.

26 And hath made of one blood all nations of men for to dwell on all the face of the earth, and hath determined the times before appointed, and the bounds of their habitation;

This Unknown God, who is the Creator of all things, needs nothing materially from His creatures. He is the Creator of mankind in particular. It is He who created all peoples and all races, "made of one blood of all nations." In other words, Paul said we are all from the same ancestral origin. Therefore, there was no justification in the claim that the Greeks were superior to other peoples, namely the barbarians; and there is no justification in the parallel beliefs today. Consequently, whether in the new creation or in the old, there is no room for the idea of racial superiority at all. The same Creator, the Almighty God, created us all equally.

Continuing the argument of creation, Paul said that God created people and placed them on earth to look after it. The idea, in this passage, is not that God created the nations and put each nation in a particular area of the earth as their own. Rather He created people to occupy the earth, the habitable areas of the earth. The national frontiers and borders are mainly man-made. The phrase "and hath determined the times before appointed," means that God even determined the different seasons before man was created and placed on earth. Paul's argument, which is consistent with the biblical narrative, was that the earth was formed and furnished to be a home for all before humans themselves were brought to occupy it. The boundaries "of their habitation" does not mean national geographical boundaries (Deuteronomy 32:8), but boundaries of human existence. The land, as opposed to the sea, for example, was just as He allotted them for "fruitful seasons" (Acts 14:17).

27 That they should seek the Lord, if haply they might feel after him, and find him, though he be not far from every one of us:

In verse 27, Paul spelled out the chief goal of God's dealing with human beings: that they seek Him, with the hope "that they might feel after him, and find him." To feel (Greek *pselaphao*) after the Lord has the idea of "groping" or searching, as in the dark, as one groping in the dark for the telephone. This is what people today and the Athenians were doing, groping for the true God—the Unknown God. This confirms the fact that man, as a religious being, is always searching. Paul writes to the Romans and says in Romans 1:20-21:

For since the creation of the world God's invisible qualities— his eternal power and divine nature—have been clearly seen, being understood from what has been made, so that men are without excuse. For although they knew God, they neither glorified him as God nor gave thanks to him, but their thinking became futile and their foolish hearts were darkened. (NIV)

It is because of this groping that we have so many religions and cults. People, however, have been groping in the wrong areas, as if God is too far and out of reach. Paul says that God is near, and that whoever seeks Him with his heart will find Him—"feel" Him. Therefore, it is senseless to try to house the divine in material sanctuaries, worship Him with material goods, or represent Him with stone, wood, or images of any other material. Unfortunately, people do not realize how near God is to those who diligently seek Him.

28 For in him we live, and move, and have our being; as certain also of your own poets have said, For we are also his offspring. 29 For as much then as we are the offspring of God, we ought

not to think that the Godhead is like unto gold, or silver, or stone, graven by art and man's device.

Paul illustrates his argument about the proximity of the divine with two quotations from their own poets, which, in part, say, "For in him we live, and move, and have our being" and that "we are also his offspring." According to various sources, the first poem is attributed to Epimenides the Cretan poet, and the second to Aratus of Cilicia in praise of Zeus from Greek philosophy. Paul is definitely not trying to compare Zeus with the God and Father of our Lord Jesus Christ, but he is trying to point out to the Athenians the futility of their religion. Indirectly, Paul indicates that the true God, which is unknown to them, and whom they worship (*eusebeo*) ignorantly is the real source of life and the One who, as well, sustains life, not Zeus. Since we are the offspring (*genos*) of God, (not in the same sense as the stoic philosophers), Paul contended, it did not make sense, therefore, to think of Him in terms of crafted images of "gold, or silver, or stone," fashioned with man's (i.e., man-made) instruments. "Offspring" here refers to the biblical doctrine of man as being created in God's image and likeness. This is what we inherited from Adam, who was created by God to reproduce. In this sense, we are the offspring of God, and, therefore, we ought to worship Him and give Him the honor due Him. Honor is definitely not given to Him if man envisages the divine in terms of the listed items above. Paul concurs with Isaiah 44:9ff. (See also Psalm 115:4ff; 135:5ff).

30 And the times of this ignorance God winked at; but now commandeth all men everywhere to repent: 31 Because he hath appointed a day, in the which he will judge the world in righteousness by that man whom he hath ordained; whereof

he hath given assurance unto all men, in that he hath raised him from the dead.
Paul presents the Gospel of repentance and calls on his audience to change, in view of the forthcoming judgment. At that time, everyone will stand to be judged according to the work they have done. Paul starts this section by giving them hope that, since they have been acting in ignorance, God has overlooked it in the past ("winked at" Greek *hupereido*, to overlook, i.e., not punished). This idea is echoed in Romans 3:25. Although He overlooked the past because they have acted in ignorance, God demands a change through repentance. He can justly demand repentance because of the provision He made by the advent and the work of Christ. Without Him, there is no other hope of escaping divine judgment (Luke 13:3). The call for repentance is for "all men (mankind) everywhere."

This invitation is universal just as the gift (John 3:16) and the judgment are universal. We are all created by God, and we are equal before Him. He does not discriminate in His mercy, or in His judgment: there is no class distinction with God. Everyone will be judged. Paul says that God has set a day when he will judge the world of righteousness (Psalms 9:8; 96:13; 98:9), and the agent of the judgment has already been appointed. It is, "that man whom He God hath ordained" to fulfill God's eternal purpose (Acts 10:42). That Man is Jesus Christ, God's Son. Everyone will be judged, based on Christ's righteousness. He has given Him authority to execute judgment, because He is the Son of man (John 5:22, 27; Romans 2:16; Matthew 25:31-46). The proof and assurance of this judgment is provided in raising this Agent from the dead. Paul says that the resurrection of Christ is a guarantee for the resurrection and judgment of all men (1 Corinthians 15:1-23). It ought to be observed that Paul did not mention the name of this man. However, it is a well-known historical fact, which no one can deny. The man is Jesus. Why did Paul omit mentioning the name Jesus in the entire passage, even though it was implicitly obvious in his argument?

32 And when they heard of the resurrection of the dead, some mocked: and others said, We will hear thee again of this matter. 33 So Paul departed from among them. 34 Howbeit certain men clave unto him, and believed: among the which was Dionysius the Areopagite, and a woman named Damaris, and others with them.

Verse 32-34 is the conclusion of Paul's sermon and its result. It is said that the idea of resurrection of the dead was not agreeable to the minds of most of Paul's audience. To Epicureans and the Stoics, resurrection and judgment were not a reality. As soon as they heard about the subject of resurrection, while Paul was still speaking, the crowd broke up. Some mocked him, that is, they *chleuazo* which means to throw out the lip, to jeer. Some deferred the meeting for the future, either out of curiosity, or a gentler way of dismissing him and his teaching. Afterwards, Paul departed from there to Corinth (18:1). Nevertheless, before he left, he made some converts through his teaching. Among them, were Dionysius, who was a member of the Areopagus, a woman named Damaris, and others.

Citizens of Two Kingdoms
Based on Romans 13

DEFINING THE ISSUE

"It is a sin for you not to vote," said the pastor to his congregation.

"We paid too much in the 60's—through the marches, the protests, the sit-ins, the fire hoses, the dogs, the reproach—we paid too much for you to be able to put your 'x' on the line for you not to vote!"

This Chicago pastor was trying to get his people actively involved in the '87 mayoral election. The White candidates who aspired to the office of mayor were joining forces for the purpose of defeating the Black incumbent, Mayor Harold Washington. It was imperative that all the church members exercise their civic responsibility to vote.

Increasingly, many Black pastors and Christians are realizing the importance of becoming involved in the political and governmental affairs of life. This is especially true when certain political parties threaten the well-being and very survival of Black Americans. Black believers must become involved. Why?

Because Christians are citizens of two kingdoms—God's and "Caesar's." And if the righteousness of God's people is not brought to bear upon the governmental and political affairs of our society, then the wickedness of satanic and ungodly forces will run rampant. And this will be done with little or no regard for bringing justice and genuine relief to the powerless minorities in the society.

AIM

To motivate students to become cooperatively involved with God and His redemptive works in political, governmental, and social affairs.

SCRIPTURE TEXT

> ROMANS 13:1 Let every soul be subject unto the higher powers. For there is no power but of God: the powers that be are ordained of God.
>
> 2 Whosoever therefore resisteth the power, resisteth the ordinance of God: and they that resist shall receive to themselves damnation.
>
> 3 For rulers are not a terror to good works, but to the evil. Wilt thou then not be afraid of the power? Do that which is good, and thou shalt have praise of the same:
>
> 4 For he is the minister of God to thee for good. But if thou do that which is evil, be afraid; for he beareth not the sword in vain: for he is the minister of God, a revenger to execute wrath upon him that doeth evil.
>
> 5 Wherefore ye must needs be subject, not only for wrath, but also for conscience sake.
>
> 6 For for this cause pay ye tribute also: for they are God's ministers, attending continually upon this very thing.

7 Render therefore to all their dues: tribute to whom tribute is due; custom to whom custom; fear to whom fear; honour to whom honour.

8 Owe no man any thing, but to love one another: for he that loveth another hath fulfilled the law

9 For this, Thou shalt not commit adultery, Thou shall not kill, Thou shalt not bear false witness, Thou shall not covet; and if there be any other commandment, it is briefly comprehended in saying, namely, Thou shalt love thy neighbor as thyself.

10 Love worketh no ill to his neighbour: therefore love is the fulfilling of the law.

11 And that, knowing the time, that now it is high time to awake out of sleep: for now is our salvation nearer than when we believed.

12 The night is far spent, the day is at hand: let us therefore cast off the works of darkness, and let us put on the armour of light.

13 Let us walk honestly, as in the day; not in rioting and drunkenness, not in chambering and wantonness, not in strife and envying.

14 But put ye on the Lord Jesus Christ, and make not provision for the flesh, to fulfil the lusts thereof.

BIBLE BACKGROUND

How should a Christian relate to government? Some people say we should have nothing to do with it except to pray. Others become so involved with politics that they lose their ability to speak prophetically to political and governmental leaders. The vast majority of Christians fit somewhere between these poles.

A Christian can be involved in political and governing affairs and still be Christian if they understand God's role for governing authorities. God ordains governing authorities as an extension of His own involvement in the affairs of the world. In this sense, all governing authorities are sacred, none are secular. For they owe their existence to God Himself.

Thus, governing authorities should punish those who live wrong and reward those who live right. When those in authority fulfill this role, and only when they fulfill this role, are they acting as God's servants. So when Christians cooperate with the governing authorities who fulfill their God-given role, they are participating with God who has ordained such governance to preserve society from lawlessness and to influence people to come to Himself.

Christians also maintain high standards of integrity in their general social relationships. For one thing, Christians pay their debts. They never borrow money in order to "hustle" the lender. Instead, they do all within their ability to pay back, in a timely manner, the money they have borrowed, whether from friends or in business. In short, a Christian is financially trustworthy.

The financial trustworthiness of Christians, shown in their carefulness to repay borrowed money, flows from their fulfillment of the law of Christ's love. A Christian has a debt of love to continuously pay to all social contacts, lenders notwithstanding. And love does not do wrong to a neighbor. It is through practicing love that a child of God will fulfill God's law. And the fulfilling of God's law is a redemptive work which the society needs.

Christians must not neglect their personal conduct. For they are ultimately responsible to God for the way they live despite the political and social standards of society. Each believer lives with an understanding of the wonderful salvation of God, which has been brought forth by Christ into human existence. The realization of God's reign on earth and completion of God's plan of salvation will happen when Jesus returns.

As Paul wrote his epistle, he was very much aware that the return of Jesus was close at hand. The dawning of God's complete redemption would soon break forth into the brightness of the new day. And when it comes, believers should not be caught living the "night life." They should not participate in orgies and drunkenness, sexual immorality and indecency, or in fighting and jealousy. Such behavior is socially degenerative. Instead, Christians should put on Jesus. Jesus and His way of living is the light of God's new day.

POINTS TO PONDER

1. *All governing authorities are _____. (Romans 13:1)*
2. *A governing authority is the "minister of God" for what purpose? (v. 4)*

_____

_____

3. *Christians are to _____ except _____. (v. 8)*
4. *How near is our salvation? (v. 11)*

_____

_____

5. *Name the six sins that Christians are to cast off. (v. 13)*

_____

_____

LESSON AT-A-GLANCE

1. Being Christian in political affairs (Romans 13:1-7)
2. Being Christian in social relations (v.8-10)
3. Being Christian in personal conduct (v. 11-14)

EXPLORING THE MEANING

1. Being Christian in political affairs (Romans 13:1-7)

The command of Jesus for Christians to render to Caesar those things which are Caesar's and to God the things which are God's (Mark 12:17) shows that Christians are to be involved in governing and political affairs. It also shows that Christians should be involved in such affairs with an intent to change society. This implication is perceived when we ask the question, "What things belong to God?" The obvious answer is everything, "the earth is the Lord's, and the fulness thereof; the world and they that dwell therein" (Psalm 24:1). So even the governing and political realms belong to God. And it is with this attitude that the Christian should become involved in these affairs.

The reason emphasis is placed on submission to the governing authorities as described in verse 1 becomes apparent when we remind ourselves that society was ruled by an autocratic king, the head of a monarchy. This is why (1 Timothy 2:1ff.) Christians were urged only to pray for the governing authorities. There was little else that could be done to participate in the governing affairs of life.

All governing authorities are ordained by God. They are legally constituted bodies of society established to promote its betterment. They may take different forms (e.g., democracy, monarchy, etc.), but their divine sanction is predicated on their fulfilling their God-ordained role.

Governing authorities are to reward the righteous and punish the wicked (Romans 13:2-4). This is the essential role of government (see also 1 Peter 2:13-14; 4:15-16). And when government, of whatever kind, violates its God-ordained role, it loses its divine sanction. In such cases, Christians are called not to submit to such bankrupt government, but to "obey God rather than man" (Acts 5:29).

In the meantime, Christians are to take pains to submit to everything that is rightfully demanded—taxes, revenue, respect, honor (Romans 13:6-7)—so that when, for reasons of conscience, they must disobey governing authorities, the lines will be clearly drawn between right and wrong (v. 5).

Unlike the Roman Christians, we in America live in a democracy. We can do more than submit to an unjust government. Built into our constitution is the provision that gives us the right to petition government for redress for wrongs and work to change unjust laws. Christians can vote, protest, lobby, sue, even become conscientious objectors. We can politically organize and nominate our own candidates and sponsor referenda. In specific geographical localities, we can incorporate into smaller units that can self-govern.

Governmentally and politically speaking, the Lord would say to Christians who are His servants of preservation and change in American society, "Live as free men, but do not use your freedom as a cover-up for evil; live as servants of God" (1 Peter 2:16, NIV).

2. Being Christian in social relations (vv. 8-10)

Besides properly relating to the government, Christians also have a responsibility to live with integrity as they relate to people in general. The law which governs such behavior is the law of Christ. It is the law that teaches us to love our neighbors as we love ourselves

(13:9; cf. Leviticus 19:18; Matthew 22:37-40). The law of love is a debt to be continuously paid to people (Romans 13:8). It is to be actively fulfilled but is never completely fulfilled (v. 9).

The one area highlighted by Paul in this regard is repayment of money. He commands, "owe no man any thing" (v. 8a). And, surely, we need to hear this command in our lives during this day. There are Christians who are financial deadbeats. They are hustlers in sheep's clothing. They borrow from everybody and repay nobody, unless they are forced. They relate this way to credit companies, to stores offering charge cards, to church trustees or to the poor saints committee, to friends, to relatives, even to the naive and unsuspecting—they are really subtle con men. They borrow but have no intention of repaying.

The way a person handles money and repays what they owe is a genuine and good test of a person's "Christlikeness." "The wicked borrow and do not repay, but the righteous give generously" (Psalm 37:21).

3. Being Christian in personal conduct (vv. 11-14)

A Christian also has a personal obligation to himself which may be likened to Aretha Franklin's words, "Respect yourself."

In so many words, Paul told the Roman believers, "Respect yourself, don't let Jesus come back and catch you still turning over in bed. Wake up, get up" (see Romans 13:11). "Respect yourself. Get up, let that bed go, daylight is coming when Jesus shall arrive. Take off your nighttime clothes, the orgies, the drunkenness, the sexual immorality, the various forms of indecency, the dissension and the jealousy" (see vv. 12–13, NIV). "Respect yourself. Put on some clothes suitable for the day, even the Day of the Lord. Matter of fact, just put on the Lord Jesus Christ, and quit trying to crawl back into the darkness of sin" (see v. 14, NIV).

The message is clear. In light of the Lord's return, a Christian owes it to himself to respect himself by living like a genuine believer in Christ. If he doesn't live like a believer, a Christian will be caught with "all his stuff hanging out" when Jesus returns. And if the salvation of the saints was nearer to the Romans than when they had initially put their trust in Christ (v. 11b), how much nearer is it to us today, more than 1900 years later?

DISCERNING MY DUTY

1. *Why do you think God established government even though He knew some leaders would be corrupt?*
2. *What do you say to believers who do not pay taxes because their tax money goes to support causes they do not believe in?*
3. *What does it mean to owe nothing to anyone except to love them (Romans 13:8)?*
4. *What does Jesus' return have to do with obeying government authorities?*
5. *During the Civil Rights Movement, Black people in America took a stand against the unjust laws of the south. The bus boycott in Montgomery, Alabama, led by Dr. Martin Luther King, Jr., encouraged people to break these unjust laws in order to achieve justice. Would you agree with Dr. King's actions?*

DECIDING MY RESPONSE

Truthfully answer the following questions:

Are you a good citizen?

Do you drive the speed limit?

If you see a crime happening, do you report it?

Do you pray for politicians and the political process? Do you respect police officers?

Do you pay all of the taxes you owe to the government?

LIGHT ON THE HEAVY

It is good to catch a glimpse of the political background during the time when the Epistle of Romans was written. Christians were citizens of two kingdoms, so they had to learn how to relate to governing authorities. This would include municipal, provincial, or imperial authorities. Jesus had told His followers to render to Caesar the things that are Caesar's, and to God the things that are God's (cf. Mark 12:17).

Early on, the Roman government considered Christianity a sect of Judaism, and the imperial restrictions imposed on Jews applied to Christians as well. The founder of Christianity had been convicted and executed on a charge of sedition by the sentence of a Roman judge. The inscription placed upon His cross told the story: "The King of the Jews."

Later, Christians were accused of defying Caesar's decrees, saying there was another king, one called Jesus (see Acts 17:6-7). As Christianity began to sever its ties to Judaism, it ran into problems of its own. Everywhere Paul went to preach the Gospel, trouble seemed to always follow him—to the discredit of the Jews and the Judaizers. The principle of rendering to Caesar that which is his, Paul sought to lay before the Church at Rome.

MORE LIGHT ON THE TEXT

Romans chapter 13 is the most prominent passage in the New Testament that specifically deals with the civic responsibility of the Christian. To understand how this passage fits, one has to study the whole book of Romans. It is generally assumed that the book is divided into two main parts. Part one (chapters 1-11) is doctrinal and deals with the plan of salvation, justification by faith, and the work of the Holy Spirit in sanctification.

Part two (chapters 12-16) is practical and contains mainly exhortations and instructions concerning Christian social and civic duties. Here, Paul spells out the Christian's responsibilities to various segments of the society. In chapter 12, Paul talks about how Christians should live consecrated and separated lives in the world (v. 1-2), which is a service to God; how they are to use their spiritual gifts within the body (vv. 3-8), and live as brothers in love, humility, and unity (vv. 9-16). The last section of chapter 12 (vv. 17-21) is devoted to teaching the Christian attitude toward enemies and persecutions. Paul concludes that section with these words, "Be not overcome of evil, but overcome evil with good." Then he goes directly to the subject of the Christian's attitudes and duties to human governments and civic rulers.

As chapter 13 relates to the rest of the book, it is possible to see in verses 1-7 the application of Paul's teaching about good and evil (12:17, 21) and the call to live peaceably with everyone (12:18). In the exhortation of 12:1, 2 Paul lays the foundation of Christian service and ethics in its various forms, and this definitely includes the believer's relation to the state. Another vital point of interest in understanding this passage is its historical political environment of Roman rule. History has it that this period was a time of persecution against the Jews whom Claudius expelled from Rome (Acts 18:2). Some suggest that the Jews (including Christians) who returned to Rome after the death of Claudius became hostile and rebellious toward the state because of the way Claudius treated them. If these conclusions are correct, we can assume that Paul was giving specific instructions for a specific situation, rather than a general or universal counsel. However, the instructions here are applicable everywhere and at all times, even though they seem difficult to accept in view of the nature and standard of our government systems today.

1 Let every soul be subject unto the higher powers. For there is no power but of God: the powers that be are ordained of God. 2 Whosoever therefore resisteth the power resisteth the ordinances of God: and they that resist shall receive to themselves damnation.

Using the language of command, Paul instructed his readers (both Jewish and Gentile Christians, and in fact, everybody) to submit to "the higher powers" and gave his reasons. The grounds for this submission can be expressed under three headings:

1. Civil governments are divinely instituted (Romans 13:1-2).
2. Civil governments are commissioned to promote and preserve order (vv. 3-4).
3. Civil governments deserve our submission because of Christian conscience (vv. 5-7).

The phrase "let every soul" means every person, especially the Christians. With the use of the imperative, we hear Paul giving a command or ordinance from God. It seems that Paul was aware of the rebellion of Jewish citizens against the Roman government and was giving instruction to the Christians to submit to the governing authority.

The word "subject" is a translation of the Greek word *hupotasso*. The word means to subordinate or place oneself under someone else. Paul's choice of the word *hupotasso* here, instead of *hupakouo*, i.e., to obey, is noteworthy. To "obey" is to carry out, to fulfill a command, or to comply with an order, which seems to have a stronger meaning. One has to be subject to the government, but there could be circumstances where one must disobey a specific order of the government. When obedience to human authority clearly contradicts the divine principles and divine orders, Peter's bold statement to the Jewish council is applicable: "We ought to obey God rather than men" (Acts 5:29; compare Acts 4:19 and Galatians 1:10).

Paul probably had this idea in mind as he wrote this passage. His life and ministry is a testimony. He was proud to be a Roman citizen. But when it came to preaching the Gospel, he was uncompromising. He would rather be imprisoned than disobey the Lord's command. At the same time, he was prepared to accept the consequences of his disobedience to the Roman command, which forbade such activity. Other apostles did the same. They preferred imprisonment to freedom in order to preach the Gospel. Paul then gave the order that all must pay allegiance to the authorities, which he called "higher powers."

The Greek word *huperecho* literally means supreme powers. Different writers and translators render it as state or governing authorities. The word appears in Paul's letter to Titus (3:1), where Paul asked him, "Remind the people to be subject to the rulers and authorities, to be obedient, to be ready to do whatever is good." It is also strongly echoed by Peter as part of our civil responsibility, using the same words (1 Peter 2:13, 14). Why should they submit to the authorities? Paul unquestionably answered it thus: "For there is no power but of God: the powers that be are ordained of God" (Romans 13:1b). The word "power" (Greek *exousia*) means delegated authority and the word "ordained" (Greek *tasso*) is translated appointed or determined and to arrange in an orderly manner. It is slightly different from the Greek word *tithemi* used by Christ in John 15:16 and translated as "ordained," which is to appoint for a purpose. Probably it is better to translate *tasso* as instituted. Therefore, Paul says there is no power without God allowing it. God has the supreme authority, and He delegates power to whomever He wishes (Daniel 4:32). It is He who "sets up kings and deposes them" (Daniel 2:21). Proverbs 8:15, 16 says of wisdom, "By me kings reign, and princes decree justice. By me princes rule, and nobles, even all the judges of the earth." Jesus reminds Pilate that the power he (Pilate) has to crucify Him is from God (John 19:11).

The question that arises is "if every government or ruler is instituted or appointed by God, why are they often unjust, godless, and lack moral integrity?" The answer is clear. Although God determines human institutions, He is not responsible for their actions. They are, however, accountable for their actions just as King Saul and all the bad kings of Israel after him were all accountable for their evil reigns.

After establishing that God determines all governing authorities, Paul warns that any resistance against the authority of the state is resistance against God's ordinance, and it should be punished. Whosoever resists (Greek *antitasso*), i.e., to set oneself against; to oppose, is, in fact, resisting the plan of God in human government, which is tantamount to opposing God. Those who rebel will bring judgment upon themselves. The King James Version rendering of judgment, "damnation," seems to suggest that the Christian would lose his salvation. This understanding does not fit well with the trend of thought in this passage. The more likely understanding is that it refers to the punishment which is administered by the human authority.

Two questions arise here. What of the pacifists who refuse to become involved in wars? What about the religious groups or sects that refuse to comply with the governing orders or take part in government activities?

3 For rulers are not a terror to good works, but to the evil. Wilt thou then not be afraid of the power? do that which is good, and thou shalt have praise of the same: 4 For he is the minister of God to thee for good. But if thou do that which is evil, be afraid; for he beareth not the sword in vain: for he is the minister of God, a revenger to execute wrath upon him that doeth evil.

In this section, Paul gives the function of civil rulers: they exist to promote and preserve order in the society. Their duty is not to terrorize the people who practice good behavior, but to punish evildoers. Using a rhetorical question, Paul communicates that, in view of their enormous authority, people should "be afraid" of those in power. "Being afraid" here is to be respectful and obedient by doing what is right. Paul then qualifies the phrase by clearly admonishing his readers to "do that which is good" and reap the benefit of it, i.e., the praise of the rulers. In verse 3, Paul negatively states the duty of the rulers, they "are not a terror to good works," but in verse 4 he states the same fact positively, this time using a singular pronoun, "he is the minister of God to thee for good." The singular is used in a collective sense to mean the rulers as in verse 3.

Paul describes the secular authority twice as God's minister (Greek *diakonos*), i.e., deacon or servant, from the verb form *diakoneo*, i.e., to serve. It has the idea of one who carries the command or order of another; and it continues the concept of divine appointment, found in verse 1. Because of the language of court (judgment) and concept of law and order, some translate the word "diakonos" as "magistrate" and others as "policeman." Whichever is the case, the minister represents the government in carrying out the ordinances of God. God has delegated authority to the civil rulers to defend the good and punish the evil. What does this punishment include? Does it include capital punishment? What does Paul mean by saying, "He beareth not the sword in vain"? (v. 4).

This passage poses some other troubling questions that need to be addressed at this point. Paul's writing does not seem to take into consideration that some governments are tyrannical and evil, rewarding evil and suppressing good. According to historical records, a few years after Paul wrote this letter, Rome, under the emperor Nero, launched persecutions against the Church in which many Christians were killed. Paul himself suffered tremendous persecutions at the hands of authorities in power. It was not because of the evil they had done, but because of the Gospel, which was thought to be a threat to the Roman authorities. Slave trade in our generation (within the last century) is a case to consider. How can we justify slavery, which was approved and orchestrated by the government, as ordained of God? Was the South African government under the apartheid regime ordained by God?

How can we account for the unlawful killing of innocent people, and the injustices that prevail in our court systems, where a group of people are subtly and deliberately targeted to be victimized by the very government that is supposed to protect them? A government where the color of your skin, or accent of your language, the tribe you come from, or even your religion, determines your fate in a court of law, even before the hearing begins, is horrible. Justice is raped and hideously suppressed under such a government. How can we honestly say that such systems are ordained of God and ministering the ordinances of God?

Perhaps the best way to look at this problem is to assume that Paul was presenting the functions of an ideal government whose responsibility was to reward and encourage good and punish evil. He was presenting a government that cared for the well-being of all its citizens and protected them. It is probably based on the assumption (if accepted) where Paul warned against any rebellion and all revolutionary activities against the government. If this warning was neglected, fear would be the order, since the authority had the sword.

Another possible way to look at this problem from the scriptural and spiritual perspectives is to apply the principle of Romans 8:28, whereby God brings good out of apparent evil. Therefore, is there any room for revolution against injustices in a system of government where right and liberty are taken away from peace-loving men and women? Should Christians deny themselves their fundamental human rights and freedoms by keeping silent, then suffering because they are Christians? On the other hand, is it okay for Christians to voice their displeasure when their freedom is jeopardized and justice denied them? What method is appropriate for Christians to make known their grievances to the ruling authorities? Scripture does not support the use of violence as a means of effecting social reform, rather it tends to support peaceful reform (see Luke 22:36-38). Do we find suitable examples in the lives of Dr. Martin Luther King Jr. and Nelson Mandela, who strongly advocated peaceful revolution to fight against injustice and maltreatment for their people? They suffered and paid the penalty even with their own life and freedom.

5 Wherefore ye must needs be subject, not only for wrath, but also for conscience sake.
Paul now gives two reasons why it is necessary for the people to submit: first, for the wrath, and second, for conscience's sake. In view of the power bestowed on the governing authority to punish,

Paul said that his readers should be submissive to avoid the ultimate consequence of being punished, which sometimes, could mean death. Therefore, the fear of being punished should serve as motivation to avoid wrongdoing. Punishment, such as spanking children or imprisonment for older people, has been used as a restraining measure against doing what is bad. The aim of punishment is to make people fear and thereby avoid activities that would warrant such consequences. Therefore, Paul said that for fear of being punished, people should submit to the authority.

The other reason that Paul gives, which should motivate his listening Christians to submit to authorities, is their conscience. Here Paul says to the Christians that it is not good enough to submit simply to avoid being punished. They should do so because it is right "not only for wrath, but also for conscience sake" (Romans 13:5). "Conscience" (Greek *suneidesis*) is defined in the dictionary as the awareness of a moral or ethical aspect of one's conduct, together with the urge to prefer right over wrong. It is the feeling, which is resident in everyone, that says one is doing what is right or wrong. It is a built-in checking device for wrong and right in every one of God's created beings. Our conscience serves as a guide for our actions. Unfortunately, we often go against our conscience. The scribes and Pharisees could not stone the woman caught in adultery, because their consciences convicted them (John 8:9). Paul argued that the Gentiles, who did not have the law, were able to keep the law because they had the law written in their hearts and consciences (Romans 2:14-15). Therefore, he allowed no room for excuses for sin or wrongdoing.

Remember when Jesus said that Paul was kicking "against the pricks" during his encounter with the Lord on his way to Damascus to persecute the Church? Some interpret Christ's statement to mean that Paul was fighting against his own conscience (see

Acts 9:1-5). For Christians, the conscience, sanctified by the work of the Holy Spirit, is always a guiding principle that leads them to do right. Unbelievers and apostates may sometimes have their consciences so seared, as with a hot iron, that they cannot choose between right and wrong, or good and evil (see 1 Timothy 4:2). Paul, therefore, says that it is better to submit because our conscience says it is the right thing to do, rather than submitting merely to avoid punishment.

6 For this cause pay ye tribute also: for they are God's ministers, attending continually upon this very thing. 7 Render therefore to all their dues: tribute to whom tribute is due; custom to whom custom; fear to whom fear; honour to whom honour.

Based on conscience, Paul urged the people to pay their tributes to the government, and he gave reasons why they should: because they are ministers of God. The word "tribute" (Greek *phoros*) is translated as taxes or assessment. For the third time in this passage (v. 4), Paul maintained that the civil government and the law enforcement officer who served under the government are God's servants. Paul uses a different Greek word *leitougos*, which generally means public servant, instead of *diakonos*, (v. 4) and he uses the plural instead of the singular as in the previous verse. *Leitougos* is also used to describe one who serves in the temple or a worshiper of God. Paul places these public servants in the same category with those who minister the Word. These ministers, Paul contends, give their full time to serve, and do not have other ways to earn a living. This supports the truth that a worker is worthy of his wages (see Luke 10:7). For that reason, every good citizen ought to fulfill his or her social and civic responsibilities, which include payment of taxes.

This is also consistent with the teachings and example of Christ. Although Jesus denounced the obligation imposed by the Pharisees to pay the temple's taxes, He nonetheless never refused to pay His own taxes and His disciples' taxes (see Matthew 17:24-27; compare Matthew 22:15-22; Mark 12:13-17). Verse 7 serves to emphasize what Paul had been saying in respect to the same public service and our civic responsibility. Paul, then, using an imperative, as if giving a command, called on everyone to "render" (Greek *apodate*), i.e., "give back" to everyone what is due (owed) him or her.

The language is the same that Christ used when answering the Pharisees and scribes, when they came to ask whether it is right or not to pay tribute to Caesar (see Mark 12:14, 17). "To give back" has the idea of paying back something owed to or something received from another. Then Paul gives examples of things that can be given back to those who deserve them. They include "tributes" (*phoros*), which probably refers to direct taxation (e.g., income tax) and "customs" (Greek *telos*), which may refer to duties imposed on imported goods and merchandise, or import and export duties. The word "fear," which is a translation of *phobos*, likely means reverence and honor; "time" means respect. All these we give back to those to whom they are owed. He advises that respect be given to those in authority, not necessarily because of their good character, but because of their office. Probably, Paul's mention of "fear" tends to refer to God and "honor" to earthly rulers. Peter says, "Show proper respect to everyone: Love the brotherhood of believers, fear God and honor the king" (1 Peter 2:17).

8 Owe no man any thing, but to love one another: for he that loveth another hath fulfilled the law. 9 For this, Thou shalt not

commit adultery, Thou shalt not kill, Thou shalt not bear false witness, Thou shalt not covet; and if there be any other commandment, it is briefly comprehended in this saying, namely, Thou shalt love thy neighbour as thyself. 10 Love worketh no ill to his neighbour: therefore love is the fulfilling of the law.

After dealing with the Christian's responsibility and civil obligation to the civil authority and public servants, Paul now turns to the Christian's conduct towards his neighbor. Here he goes back to the theme of love, which he dealt with in chapter 12:9-10, and which dominates his writings—a theme that separates the Christian from the world. The connection between this section and the previous one is the use of the word "owe" which has the same root as "dues." "Owe no man any thing" does not necessarily infer that one is forbidden to borrow from or lend to people. That would contradict the teaching of mutual help Jesus advocates: "Do not turn away from the one who wants to borrow from you" (Matthew 5:42, NIV). What Paul tends to imply here is that we should not allow our debts to be delinquent or outstanding. Rephrased in a positive way, Paul says that all debts should be paid.

In reference to the foregoing section, the Christian should not withhold the payment of debts such as paying taxes, customs, respect, and reverence to the people that deserve them. Instead of owing anything to any man, the apostle says we owe mutual love to one another. Here, loving one another (not only fellow Christians, but all mankind) seems to imply that we owe it as a duty to love; it is an obligation that needs to be fulfilled, and no one can say that he or she has completely discharged this duty. Love, according to Paul, is a continuing debt that we owe to one another. There is always room to love more. "For he that loveth another hath fulfilled the law" (Romans 13:8) presents a strong truth about love, for love is the foundation on which the law is built. This strengthens and parallels Paul's statement in Romans 8:4 that the righteous requirement of the law is being fulfilled in those who "walk not after the flesh, but after the Spirit."

Galatians 5:22-23 confirms that the life of the Spirit is anchored in the fruit of love, without which, Paul says, there is no law. Keeping the law or commandment is equivalent to loving one another. In Romans 13:9, Paul defines some of the precepts of evil practices, which do not conform to the love of neighbors. These include:

1. Committing immoral acts of adultery, thereby depriving someone of his or her spouse.
2. Committing murder, thereby depriving someone of his or her life.
3. Robbing someone of his or her property by stealing.
4. Robbing someone of his or her good name by bearing false witness against the person or implicating an innocent person.
5. Coveting another person's fortune or goods, which amounts to selfish desire, which is the key that controls all other evils (see Romans 7:7-8).

Here Paul called to mind the Levitical law of relationship (Leviticus 19:18), reiterated by Christ in Matthew 22:39, and illustrated by His parable of the Good Samaritan in Luke 10:30-37. Paul said that all other commands are summed up in this one rule: "Love your neighbor as yourself" (Romans 13:9). Love is the guiding principle to living right, a controlling device that inhibits anyone with conscience, and with the indwelling Holy Spirit, from committing those evils that affect the well-being of others. Paul clearly stated the same fact in verse 10, "Love does no harm to its neighbor" (NIV). Based on this, Paul returned to the same thoughts given in verse 8. He now seems to defuse the apparent paradox between the Spirit and the keeping of the Law and its work which produces the awareness of sin.

11 And that, knowing the time, that now it is high time to awake out of sleep: for now is our salvation nearer than when we believed. 12 The night is far spent, the day is at hand: let us therefore cast off the works of darkness, and let us put on the armour of light.

Paul reinforced the call for love by alerting Christians to the brevity of time before Christ's return. Since the time is near, they ought to keep the law, which means loving one another. In a number of other passages, Paul wrote that the return of Christ should be a motivation for Christian living (see Philippians 4:4-7; 1 Thessalonians 5; Hebrew 10:24 ff). This is reinforced by Peter (1 Peter 4:7-11), and by James (James 5:7-11). He admonished that in view of the imminent return of Christ, believers should be alert and wake up from sleep. Although he did not know the time, Paul reminded them that each moment that passed drew "our salvation…nearer than when we first believed."

The Bible talks about three phases of our salvation. The first occurs the moment one accepts Jesus as Saviour and Lord (see Ephesians 2:8). The second is the sanctifying work of the Spirit, which occurs daily as we submit ourselves to His control (see John 17:17; 1 Corinthians 15:2; 1 Peter 1:5). The third is futuristic, when one's salvation shall be completed at the return of Christ, which Paul alluded to here (compare 1 Peter 1:9). Knowing that the time for the full realization of the redemption was at hand, "the night is far spent, the day is at hand," Paul exhorts Christians to wake up to their calling.

What does this phrase mean? It means that our present imperfect and trouble-filled life, full of temptations and difficulties, is almost over; the day of hope and blessing, of eternal life, is about to dawn upon us. With this in mind, Paul urged them to do the following things. Metaphorically speaking, they were to "cast off the works of darkness" as in putting off clothes (or garments) which were associated with evil, and in its place to put on the "armour of light," which is analogous with good deeds. The armour (Greek *hoplon*), i.e., a weapon (of war) or instrument of light, suggests that leading a good and fruitful Christian life involves warfare with the powers of darkness (see 1 Thessalonians. 5:8; Ephesians 6:12-13). Such weapons included "touches, lanterns…" (John 18:3), which showed light in the dark; and Paul referred to them as instruments of righteousness (Romans 6:13).

Most mischievous activities are always done under the cover of darkness. Therefore, light is needed to expose them. Paul contended that "the weapons of our warfare are not carnal, but mighty through God to the pulling down of strong holds" (2 Corinthians 10:4). As children of light, equipped with the armour of light, believers who have been transformed wait patiently for the *parousia*, the coming of the Lord. The term "cast off (put off)… put on" is said to represent a tradition for baptism in which the stripping and re-clothing is practiced to signify a change into a new life from the old (Ephesians 4:22ff). This is probably why early missionaries to Africa instituted the idea of wearing white garments during baptism. The missionaries replaced the African traditional names, which are usually meaningful, with English or biblical names such as "Aloysius," or "Lambert," or "Graves," etc., which oftentimes do not make sense. It is not the outer garment that Paul is advocating here; rather, it is the inner (spiritual) garment of righteousness that we are to put on.

13 Let us walk honestly, as in the day: not in rioting and drunkenness, not in chambering and wantonness, not in strife and envying. 14 But put ye on the Lord Jesus Christ, and make not provision for the flesh, to fulfill the lusts thereof.

With this spiritual garment on, we are to conduct ourselves as in the day. Paul contrasts night and day as in verse 12 where he contrasts darkness and light. It also continues the thought of the nearness of the Day of the Lord. The contrasts are also found in a number of other passages of Scripture (see Isaiah 9:2; 42:6ff; 60:1ff; Luke 16:8; John 3:19ff; Acts 26:18; 2 Corinthians 6:14; Ephesians 5:8; 1 Thessalonians 5:4ff). The overriding principle here is that we are to walk honestly as in the day, where everything is made bare to the view of everyone. Walking "honestly," (Greek euschemonos) translated becoming, properly, or decently, means that we carry ourselves in a decent and orderly manner, so as not to bring shame in the eyes of the world (1 Corinthians 14:40; 1 Thessalonians 4:11, 12). There is, therefore, no place for indecent behaviors such as rioting (*komos*), associated with unchristian partying and drunkenness (*methe*), or chambering (*koite*), associated with whoredoms or prostitution, and all kinds of uncleanness and wantonness (*aslyeia*), also translated as "lasciviousness" and refers to all types of sexual perversion.

The last set of behaviors that is forbidden for those who walk in the day include strife and envy or jealousy. Paul, in other places, warns against such practices and those who engage in them will not inherit the kingdom of God (see 1 Corinthians 6:9). Concluding this portion of the letter, Paul returns to the figure of putting on the garment (v. 12), which here is personified by the person of Christ. Using the prepositional conjunction "But," Paul contrasts the foregoing section with the imperative "put on Christ." That means that those who put on Christ have no room for such evil practices mentioned above because they have mortified "the deeds of the body" (Romans 8:13). To be clothed with a person means to take upon one the interest of another; to enter into his way of thinking and be wholly on one's side; to imitate someone in all things. To be clothed with Christ is to be like Him and assume His person and character in daily life (see Galatians 5:24; 2 Corinthians 5:17-18; Romans 6:1-14; 8:1-13); it is to be engrafted in Him (John 15) and to love and honor Him as Lord of our lives. It is allowing Him to control every aspect our being, our thoughts, actions, and our future.

Paul then summed it up by saying that, when Christ is put on, there is no provision for the works of the flesh (see Galatians 5:19-21; Romans 1:21-32; 1 Corinthians 6:9-11; Colossians 3:5-10), which contradict the works of the Spirit.

The Lord's Supper
Based on 1 Corinthians 11:17-34

DEFINING THE ISSUE

Richard and Louise gave a love feast in their home a few weeks ago. Many people gathered for the festivities, to eat, fellowship, and generally enjoy themselves. Though it was a grand time for everyone, Richard and Louise were saddened by the conduct of some of their wealthy and influential guests, who used their influence to get the best seats and food at the party.

"How could those people be so insensitive," said Richard. "There was plenty of room and food for everyone. They didn't have to push people aside to get what they wanted. All they had to do was ask."

Sometimes people who have a lot of influence and clout feel it is necessary to push around others who are less fortunate than they are. How sad that people allow their influence and prestige to go to their heads. If more people understood that God does not respect one person over another, they would treat others as they would want to be treated.

This study focuses on the Lord's Supper. Paul stressed that there is a proper manner for people to approach the Lord's table. It is not a time for self-indulgence but self-reflection.

AIM

By the end of the class period, students will be able to explain the spiritual meaning of the Lord's Supper.

SCRIPTURE TEXT

1 CORINTHIANS 11:17 Now in this that I declare unto you I praise you not, that ye come together not for the better, but for the worse.

18 For first of all, when ye come together in the church, I hear that there be divisions among you; and I partly believe it.

19 For there must be also heresies among you, that they which are approved may be made manifest among you.

20 When ye come together therefore into one place, this is not to eat the Lord's supper.

21 For in eating everyone taketh before the other his own supper: and one is hungry, and another is drunken.

22 What? have ye not houses to eat and to drink in? or despise ye the church of God, and shame them that have not? What shall I say to you? shall I praise you in this? I praise you not.

23 For I have received of the Lord that which also I delivered unto you. That the Lord Jesus the same night in which he was betrayed took bread:

24 And when he had given thanks, he brake it, and said, Take, eat: this is my body, which is broken for you: this do in remembrance of me.

25 After the same manner also he took the cup, when he had supped, saying, This cup is the new testament in my blood: this do ye, as oft as ye drink it, in remembrance of me.

26 For as often as ye eat this bread, and drink this cup, ye do show the Lord's death till he come.

27 Wherefore whosoever shall eat this bread, and drink this cup of the Lord, unworthily, shall be guilty of the body and blood of the Lord.

28 But let a man examine himself, and so let him eat of that bread, and drink of that cup.

29 For he that eateth and drinketh unworthily, eateth and drinketh damnation to himself, not discerning the Lord's body.

30 For this cause many are weak and sickly among you, and many sleep.

31 For if we would judge ourselves, we should not be judged.

32 But when we are judged, we are chastened of the Lord, that we should not be condemned with the world.

33 Wherefore, my brethren, when ye come together to eat, tarry one for another.

34 And if any man hunger, let him eat at home; that ye come not together unto condemnation. And the rest will I set in order when I come.

BIBLE BACKGROUND

Paul's first letter to the Corinthian church was prompted by reports of problems that existed within the body. The reports came from some members of the church who were part of the household of Chloe (1:11), followed by a letter from the church (7:1) probably brought by a delegation (16:17). The reports and letter raised a number of theological and practical questions which Paul addressed. Among the problems were divisions in the church, some serious doctrinal and ethical sins, and misconduct in worship. One area of misconduct was that of disunity and disharmony around the table of the Lord where the people gathered for a fellowship meal. Apparently the wealthy and influential members of the church were consuming the food and not sharing with the poor and widows of the church. The apostle wanted to correct this. He realized that the Lord's Supper was not a time for dissension but for unity. Therefore, Paul wrote to correct the problem before it destroyed the church.

POINTS TO PONDER

1. *What was the Apostle Paul concerned about? (1 Corinthians 11:18-19)*

   _____

   _____

2. *How were the believers abusing the Lord's table? (vv. 21-22)*

   _____

   _____

3. *When people partake of the Lord's Supper what are they doing? (v. 26) Explain what this means.*

   _____

   _____

4. What did Paul exhort the people to do? (v. 28)

_____

_____

5. What does it mean when a person partakes of the Lord's Supper in an unworthy manner? (v. 29)

_____

_____

LESSON AT-A-GLANCE

1. Divisions in the church (1 Corinthians 11:17-22)
2. Instructions on the Lord's Supper (vv. 23-26)
3. Problems associated with Communion (vv. 27-34)

EXPLORING THE MEANING

1. Divisions in the church (1 Corinthians 11:17-22)

Having just begun his discussion on public worship and the behavior of women in the Corinthian church (vv. 2-16), Paul turned his attention to another problem plaguing the church: the conduct of Christians during the Lord's Supper.

Paul could not commend the church on their conduct regarding their practice of worship. Instead of bringing the church together, it was actually causing a split among the members. People could not see eye-to-eye with one another and, as a result, they allowed their feelings to spill over into the service.

The divisiveness was due in part to economic reasons. The leaders were quick to acknowledge the rich and influential of the church over the poor, widows, and orphans. Instead of coming together to eat the Lord's Supper, the rich would eat and drink to their heart's content while the poor went hungry (see v. 21).

Paul was disappointed by these events. If the Corinthians did not want to share with one another, and wanted to have a private love feast, they should eat at home. By coming to the church and acting in a divisive manner, they were actually bringing shame on the church of God and on their brothers and sisters. Paul did not believe this was proper, and he scolded the people for their actions.

Ryrie states that the early Christians held a love feast in connection with the Lord's Supper, during which the people gathered for a fellowship meal, sent and received communications from other churches, and collected money for widows and orphans. Apparently, some of the wealthier members were not sharing their food, but greedily consuming it before the poor arrived at the feast.

A spirit of divisiveness should never be allowed in a church. It will destroy a ministry and eventually the people. God has called His people to unity and peace, not to disunity and disharmony.

2. Instructions on the Lord's Supper (vv. 23-26)

Paul reminded the church of what he had received from the Lord Jesus. Whether Jesus divinely communicated to the apostle about the Lord's Supper or Paul learned from others we don't know, but see MORE LIGHT ON THE TEXT below. The apostle reminded the church of the momentous occasion when Jesus Christ broke bread and drank from the cup with His disciples during the Last Supper before Calvary.

Paul reminded the church that Jesus' Last Supper happened on the night of His betrayal by one of His followers. The bread, eaten that night and served at every Last Supper since, represented Jesus' body which had been given for the sins of the world. Then Jesus took the cup which represented His blood which was shed for the remission of sins. The blood also represents a new covenant, or a new relationship by which God receives us to Himself based on faith in Jesus Christ whose blood covers our sins. Jesus reminded His followers, and us, that every time we partake of the Lord's Supper, we should remember His atoning work on the Cross and the fact that God accepted His Son's perfect sacrifice on our behalf.

Therefore, Paul stated: "As often as ye eat this bread, and drink this cup, ye do show the Lord's death till he come" (v. 26). In other words, the Lord's Supper is a visible sermon, looking back on Christ's life and death and looking forward to His second coming. Whenever we partake of the Lord's Supper, we celebrate His life, death, and return.

There is no prescribed timetable for celebrating the Lord's Supper. Most churches celebrate every first Sunday of the month. Some churches celebrate every Sunday. Jesus did not give us a prescribed timetable either. But every time we celebrate the Lord's Supper, we should do so reverently and with a sense of joy that we are part of His family because of Jesus' life and death.

3. Problems associated with Communion (vv. 27-34)

The apostle continued his exhortation by affirming that the people's behavior was unacceptable to the Lord. Those who partook of the Lord's Supper in an irreverent or unholy manner would actually be considered guilty of sinning against the body and blood of Jesus Christ. In other words, we must look inwardly to see whether there is sin in our lives, or whether we have something against another person. If we do, we must confess to the Lord immediately before we partake of the Lord's Supper.

The Apostle Paul exhorted the church to examine themselves to see whether they should partake of the Lord's Supper. After all, the rich were taking advantage of the poor in the Corinthian church and the Lord disapproved.

Self-examination is the responsibility all believers have to see whether they are in a right relationship with the Lord. If not, all that is needed is that sin be confessed and renounced, and God will cleanse us from all unrighteousness (see 1 John 1:9). Those who partake of the Lord's table without confessing their sins actually bring judgment and condemnation on themselves. In Paul's day, and ours, this may include physical sickness and even death. That's why it is so important not to take the Lord's Supper lightly. It is a powerful remembrance of what the Lord Jesus Christ has done for us.

When we partake, we proclaim that we are God's and He is our Father. It is a time of retrospection and reflection and we should do all we can to promote unity in the body through this memorial occasion.

DISCERNING MY DUTY

1. *Why is it so important that divisiveness stay out of a church?*
2. *Why were the rich unconcerned about the poor in the Corinthian church?*
3. *Why should we examine ourselves before taking the Lord's Supper?*
4. *How does one eat and drink damnation to oneself in partaking the Lord's Supper?*
5. *How can we combat or get rid of the divisiveness in churches and communities that causes groups to be against one another?*

DECIDING MY RESPONSE

This week, take an introspective look at yourself to see whether there are areas you need to give to the Lord before partaking of the

Lord's Supper. As you come to the table, reflect on its significance and spiritual meaning for your life. Don't forget to thank the Lord for His sacrifice.

LIGHT ON THE HEAVY

Feasts. The feasts, or sacred festivals, held an important place in Jewish religion. They were religious services accompanied by demonstrations of joy. Their occurrences, except for the two instituted after the exile, were fixed by divine appointment. Their purpose was to promote the community's spiritual interests. The people met in holy fellowship for acts and purposes of sacred worship. They met before God in holy assemblies (*The Zondervan Pictorial Bible Dictionary*, 1967, pp. 280-81).

MORE LIGHT ON THE TEXT

1 Corinthians 11:17: Now in this that I declare unto you I praise you not, that ye come together not for the better, but for the worse. 18 For first of all, when ye come together in the church, I hear that there be divisions among you; and I partly believe it. 19 For there must be also heresies among you, that they which are approved may be made manifest among you.

The misconduct was reported as abuse during the celebration of the "love meal" and the Lord's Supper, which occupies a large portion of our study (1 Corinthians 11:20-34). In verses 17-19, Paul deplored the people's attitude when they came together, and said that their gatherings "do more harm than good." Rather than being united in their meetings, they caused divisions, especially during their love meals and Lord's Supper (vv. 20ff, NIV).

20 When ye come together therefore into one place, this is not to eat the Lord's supper.
Here Paul begins to deplore the attitude of the people when they gather for the Lord's Supper, and says angrily, "It is not the Lord's Supper you eat" (v. 20, NIV). This sentence serves as an introduction to what is about to follow, and as a transition to his thought in verse 18, which is "interrupted" by verse 19. The phrase, "When ye come together" with "therefore" resumes the argument in verse 18 about the division, which is reported to him. The phrase "come together…into one place" means the same as in verse 18 (come together in the church). Paul says in effect, "because of the disturbing report of division caused by your selfish attitude and unmannered behavior (which he explains next), when you assemble for supper, it is not the Lord's Supper you are celebrating. It has ceased to be the Lord's supper; the spiritual significance of it is lost."

21 For in eating everyone taketh before the other his own supper: and one is hungry, and another is drunken.
Paul then explains the deplorable behavior (i.e., "everyone taketh before the other his own supper: and one is hungry, and another is drunken"), which is the main cause of the "divisions" (v. 18), and why their meal is no more to be regarded as the Lord's Supper (v. 20). The idea is that when the members come together for meals, probably social dinners which differ from the Lord's instituted "Supper," each person brings food to share and eat together. Celebration of the Lord's Supper probably follows the feast. This type of meal, called "the agape" (love) feast (Jude 12), was common among the early Christians, and an offshoot of the practice of the early church (Acts 2:42ff). It also followed the pattern of the public feast among the Jews and Greeks, in which food was

brought for everyone to share. The Corinthian Christians carried this social custom into the church. This is the same idea with the contemporary "pot luck" dinner practiced in many modern churches today. Some call it the "bring and share" dinner.

This custom is also common in some non-Christian cultures among the Igbos of Nigeria, especially among the *okonko,* an initiation society for boys who reach the age of manhood. During this ceremony, each man brings food to the city squire (*ama ala*), and everyone partakes together. This is the only time in the Igbo culture in which age is totally disregarded. The Igbos have great respect for age and older people. Part of that respect is to give preference to people who are older, e.g., allowing them first choice in everything, both in family and the public gatherings. During this feast, except when one has reported sick and unable to attend, the members present will wait until everyone gathers before they start sharing the food, and each person, whether old or young, receives an equal amount of food.

It seems this was not the case with the Corinthian church. Rather, as Paul describes it, when they gathered for supper, "everyone taketh before the other his own supper: and one is hungry, and another is drunken." There are two possible ways to look at this problem. First, there seemed to be two distinct groups within the Corinthians, as it is in every society, the rich and the poor. The rich, who brought more food, would not wait for the rest but would go ahead and eat their meals. The second possible scenario is that, when they gathered, they formed cliques, whereby the rich divided the food inequitably, to ensure that the rich received the lion's share, while the poor went without and hungry. Paul's use of "drunken" (Greek *methuo*), i.e., to be drunken; intoxicated, especially with wine, can be interpreted in two ways. Paul was either describing how gorged they were with food and that could be equated with drunkenness, or that they were actually drunk with wine. Wine is customarily part of the Jewish and ancient Eastern menu. It was not, therefore, out of place to have wine as part of the meal during the feast. Paul is then saying that the rich drank so much wine, without consideration of the "others," that they got drunk. The second explanation is probably better, since in all references in the New Testament, the word *methuo* never refers to food, but wine (Matthew 24:49; Acts 2:15; 1 Thessalonians 5:7).

22 What? Have ye not houses to eat and to drink? Or despise ye the church of God, and shame them that have not? What shall I say to you? Shall I praise you in this? I praise you not.
Paul saw this situation as so deplorable, unchristian, and inconsiderate, that he posed a series of rhetorical questions for the members. The single word, "what" that begins verse 22 seems to dramatically describe how surprised and appalled Paul was to hear this report of misconduct within the church. He seems to ask, "Is what I am hearing really true?" Stated in a different way, "I cannot believe what I am hearing!" Of course, he believed the report to be true (v. 18). By asking, "Have ye not houses to eat and to drink?" Paul tends to reduce the overindulgence to the same level of shame that is being brought upon the poor. The question is ironic. Paul responds directly to verse 21 by asking, "Is it true that you do not have homes where you can eat and drink as you please?" The obvious answer of course is, "Yes, we do." The natural response would be, "Then why do you come into the public to eat in such a selfish and greedy manner?" The second question follows the first, "Or despise ye the church of God, and shame them that have not?" By this question, Paul defines the twofold nature of their behavior, i.e., they are despising the church and humiliating (shaming) the poor. The word "despise" in (Greek *kataphroneo*)

means to think against, or to disesteem. The first part of the second question rhetorically put, can either mean: "Don't you know that by your behavior you are giving outsiders a cause to think bad about the church and, therefore, ridicule the church?" Or "Do you not know that your attitude affects the church?"

The other possible alternative to understanding this question (combining the first and second parts), is to rephrase it thus, "Do you think that by behaving the way you do, you are honoring the church and the poor?" Without waiting for the answer, Paul would say, "No. You are rather disgracing yourselves." In this case, he reverses the shame back to them, as we have discussed above. The word "shame" is from the Greek word *kataischunu* from the same root word *kata* which means down or against as in *kataphroneo* (despise) above. In this context, it means to look down upon someone, i.e., to disgrace, dishonor, or to put to blush. Either way, Paul is saying that although their actions are both a disgrace to the church and humiliating to the less privileged, the real disgrace is for them. They behaved as people who lacked proper home training and etiquette. They demonstrated a lack of self-control.

The foregoing set of questions appears with another set of rhetorical questions and with a definite negative, but firm, answer: "What shall I say to you? Shall I praise you in this? I praise you not." Paul continued to show his frustration and disappointment with them. He posed the question for their self-evaluation. The phrase, "What shall I say to you," showed Paul's displeasure. He was so surprised that he did not know what to say to them again. "Shall I praise you in this" brings in the argument in verse 17. The natural answer is, "Certainly not." In the language of verse 17, these things disqualify them for the Lord's Supper and result in sickness and sometimes death (v. 27-30).

23 For I have received of the Lord that which also I delivered unto you, that the Lord Jesus the same night in which he was betrayed took bread:
After dealing with the disappointing behavior of the church members at the love feast meal which preceded the Lord's Supper, Paul reminded them again of the historical background of the Lord's Supper and the guidelines and conditions for taking it. The essential point is that there are consequences for eating the Lord's Supper in an unworthy manner. The other point explains how to prevent such consequences.

Paul starts by first declaring the authenticity of his argument concerning the Lord's Supper and the source for his teaching. As if defending his apostolic authority again, as in Galatians 1:12 (compare Galatians 2:2; Ephesians 3:3), Paul tells them that his teaching is a direct revelation from Christ Himself. It is the same revelation and doctrine which he had already taught them earlier after founding the church. Since this tradition is not being followed, or indeed is being abused, Paul seems compelled to repeat the actual words in order to remind them of its significance. Paul says that what he is about to say is a historical fact. That is, in the same night "in which" Jesus was "betrayed He took bread" and gave thanks and gave it to the disciples. He reminds these thoughtless Corinthians of the setting (of the stage) of the Lord's Supper. He says that the institution of the Lord's Supper took place in the very same night that Jesus was "betrayed" (Greek *paradidomi*) and delivered and handed over to the soldiers. He was given up to them (John 18:30; Acts 3:13; Romans 8:32). Verse 23 repeats this historical fact.

Why was Paul recounting the whole event here? The answer could be that he was following, as one writer points out, the Jewish tradition of the Passover liturgy in which the head of the family recounts the history of past national events in order to remind each participant that he has some continuity in the body of those events. However, the next three verses carry crucial spiritual undertones for the whole situation.

24 And when he had given thanks, he brake it, and said, Take, eat: this is my body, which is broken for you, this do in remembrance of me. 25 After the same manner also he took the cup, when he had supped, saying, This cup is the new testament in my blood: this do ye as oft as ye drink it, in remembrance of me. 26 For as often as ye eat this bread, and drink this cup, ye do shew the Lord's death till he come.

Continuing the narrative, Paul points out that Jesus, after giving thanks, breaks the bread and gives it out. Jesus has the habit of giving thanks before meals, e.g., during the feeding of the 5,000 (John 6:11; compare Matthew 14:19; Mark 6:41; Luke 9:16) and at the Last Supper (Matthew 26:26). The most significant words are Christ's words as He gives out the bread. First, "Take, eat: this is my body, which is broken for you." It represents a symbol of the sacrificial body of Christ to the church. Just as the bread is broken, the body of Jesus is broken for the redemption of sins. As the Christian takes the bread, he is reminded of the death of Christ, not only as a past event, but also as a present reality.

The phrase "This is my body" does not mean the real presence of Jesus Christ is in the bread, as some doctrines assert. It does, however, maintain that in a sense the participant is confronted with the death of Christ for himself or herself (see Isaiah 52:14; 53:4-5; 1 Peter 2:24). "This do in remembrance of me" explains the purpose of the institution of the Lord's Supper, that it is a memorial of Christ. The Lord's Supper serves as a reminder of the most significant event in history, whereby Christ died to save the world. It is a memorial not of His life, but His death (v. 26) which carries redemptive value.

The cup (the wine) in like manner serves the same purpose as the bread, but represents the blood of Christ that was spilled on the cross. It symbolizes the cleansing and remission of sins (see Matthew 26:28; Ephesians 1:7; Colossians 1:20). The "cup," used figuratively for its contents, symbolizes Jesus' blood that seals the New Covenant, which is based on a better promise (See Hebrews 8:6; 9:15-22). This replaces the Old Covenant that God made with Israel. "The new testament in my blood," means a new covenant that God made with His people. "Testament" is a translation of the Greek word *diatheke*, which means a contract or covenant. Paul adds, "This do ye as oft as ye drink it, in remembrance of me," which means that the Lord's Supper ought to be observed as frequently as possible. The Bible does not specify how often. However, the early church observed it either daily (Acts 2:46) or weekly (Acts 20:7). Most churches today practice the Lord's Supper monthly. The real message is that every time we observe the Lord's Supper, we ought to show respect in proclaiming the Lord's death till He comes (v. 26, Luke 22:19). To "show forth" His death, is to keep the significance and purpose of the death of Christ afresh in our minds until His second coming (see John 14:3; Acts 1:11). The Corinthian church lost sight of the importance of this event with their greedy and selfish behavior, and therefore needed to be reminded.

27 Wherefore whosoever shall eat this bread, and drink this cup of the Lord, unworthily, shall be guilty of the body and blood of the Lord. 28 But let a man examine himself, and so let him eat of that bread, and drink of that cup.

After recounting the significance of the Lord's Supper, Paul then warns them of the consequences of partaking of the Supper in an unworthy manner. "Wherefore" (therefore), for the reasons given above (i.e., the significance of the Lord's Supper), whoever takes it unworthily (Greek *anavios*) shall be guilty of sinning against the blood and body of Christ. *Anxios* means irreverent or disrespectful. Paul calls for personal self-examination before one takes the Supper in order to avoid eating it in sin. "To examine" (Greek *dokimazo*) oneself is to put oneself to the test concerning the attitude of one's heart, one's conduct, one's behavior toward others, and one's understanding of the true purpose and nature of the Supper. Paul, in another passage, calls the Corinthians to examine their faith (2 Corinthians 13:5). According to Paul's argument, it is better not to take the Supper at all if one is not fit, than to take it in an unworthy manner.

29 For he that eateth and drinketh unworthily, eateth and drinketh damnation to himself, not discerning the Lord's body. 30 For this cause many are weak and sickly among you, and many sleep.

In Verse 29, Paul gives the reason for self-examination: "For he that eateth and drinketh unworthily, eateth and drinketh damnation (i.e., passes judgment) to himself, not discerning the Lord's body." The word discerning, translated by some as recognizing, is the Greek word *diakrino* which speaks of separating or distinguishing from. By not discerning (not distinguishing) the Lord's body, Paul speaks of their failure to distinguish between the food of the Lord's Supper and the common food of their private meal or the love feast. Alternatively, it may refer to their failure to recognize the Lord's body, that is, reflecting on His death as they eat. Another interpretation tends to be closer to Paul's idea, because of the parallel between verses 27 and 29, assuming that "the Lord's body" (v. 29) is an abridged form of "the body and blood of the Lord" (v. 27).

There is yet another possible interpretation here. "Not discerning the Lord's body" could mean their failure to recognize the distinctive nature of the church, the body of Christ. This unique nature of the body is demonstrated in the Lord's Supper, symbolized by the common table with one loaf of bread and one cup, they proclaim that through the death of Christ the church is one body. Not recognizing the Lord's body is equivalent to making light of the death of Christ, which is for the redemption of the church and would also incur God's judgment. "For this cause" refers to the result of "not discerning the Lord's body." The effect is being seen among them: "Many become weak and sickly, and some fall asleep" (i.e., die). The Greek verb *koimao* means to fall asleep and sometimes refers to physical sleep (as in Mark 14:37; Luke 22:45), but often as a euphemistic figure of speech for the word "dying" (compare John 11:11-14; 1 Corinthians 15:51; Acts 7:60).

31 For if we would judge ourselves, we should not be judged. 32 But when we are judged, we are chastened of the Lord, that we should not be condemned with the world.

In verses 31 and 32, Paul gives the purpose of the self-examination, which is to come to the Lord's table with a pure and clean heart. Paul uses the first-person plural, including himself, and gives further reason why we have to examine ourselves before approaching the table of the Lord's Supper. In verse 31, Paul, using the theme of self-examination from verse 28 and the verb "discern" (*diakrino*) from verse 29, says that if the church at Corinth had been discerning themselves, the judgment of verse 30 would not have happened. However, he adds that what they are experiencing presently is God's judgment and should be understood as "fatherly discipline" (Hebrews 12:5-8; compare Proverbs 3:11-12.) This type of discipline is necessary, Paul seems to say, since it will result in repentance, that the believer will not suffer final damnation (eternal judgment) as the rest of the unsaved world (See Revelation 20:12-15).

33 Wherefore, my brethren, when ye come together to eat, tarry one for another. 34 And if any man hunger, let him eat at home; that ye come not together unto damnation. And the rest will I set in order when I come.

Paul goes back to the problem that started the whole theological argument, the agape meal (verse 21-22), and deals with it in a positive and gentler way. Referring to the Corinthians as brethren, Paul admonishes them to be a "caring community," to show concern and respect for every member. One of the practical ways to do this is by being considerate and waiting for others when they gather to feast. He concludes by offering an alternative to deal with the problem and suggests that if anyone wants to eat sumptuously, he or she should do that at home and not in a public gathering. This will help to avert the judgment of the Lord. This portion is addressed to the members of the Corinthian church; however, it is relevant to any community of believers anywhere and at all times. Paul closes this section of the letter with a promise to set the rest of the things in order when he visits the Corinthians. Some of the important things to learn from this passage include how we as believers should relate to one another in the church; as a community of believers, we should not think only about ourselves, but about others. We should treat everyone equally in the body of Christ, both the "haves" and the "have nots." It teaches us the proper interpretation of the Lord's Supper, and the Christian's proper attitude at the Lord's table.

Working for Reconciliation
Based on 2 Corinthians 5:11-21

DEFINING THE ISSUE

Once, a story concerning a young girl who had been mistakenly separated from her biological mother at birth dominated the American media. The mother later found out that her baby, now age 14, was switched at birth, and she wanted her child. The case went to court where the young girl was forced to make a decision. The young girl claimed that she loved her adoptive parents and wanted to stay with them. She wanted nothing to do with her biological parents. After the courts had legalized her decision, she went back home to live with her adoptive parents. A few months later, she ran away from home. She decided that she wanted to be reconciled with her biological parents.

Of course, this was a happy day for her biological parents. Their daughter had come home to live with them. All the negative things she said about them in court were forgotten. These remarks were not held against her, and their relationship was restored. In our lesson today, Paul reminds us that God reconciled us to Himself and sent us out as ministers of reconciliation.

AIM

By the end of the lesson, students will be able to clearly express the message of reconciliation and the importance of what God has accomplished through the life, death, and resurrection of Jesus Christ; and will be challenged to share the message of God's love with at least one person.

SCRIPTURE TEXT

> 2 CORINTHIANS 5:11 Knowing therefore the terror of the Lord, we persuade men; but we are made manifest unto God; and I trust also are made manifest in your consciences.
>
> 12 For we commend not ourselves again unto you, but give you occasion to glory on our behalf, that ye may have somewhat to answer them which glory in appearance, and not in heart.
>
> 13 For whether we be beside ourselves, it is to God: or whether we be sober, it is for your cause.
>
> 14 For the love of Christ constraineth us; because we thus judge, that if one died for all, then were all dead:
>
> 15 And that he died for all, that they which live should not henceforth live unto themselves, but unto him which died for them, and rose again.
>
> 16 Wherefore henceforth know we no man after the flesh: yea, though we have known Christ after the flesh, yet now henceforth know we him no more.

17 Therefore if any man be in Christ, he is a new creature: old things are passed away; behold, all things are become new.

18 And all things are of God, who hath reconciled us to himself by Jesus Christ, and hath given to us the ministry of reconciliation;

19 To wit, that God was in Christ, reconciling the world unto himself, not imputing their trespasses unto them; and hath committed unto us the word of reconciliation.

20 Now then we are ambassadors for Christ, as though God did beseech you by us: we pray you in Christ's stead, be ye reconciled to God.

21 For he hath made him to be sin for us, who knew no sin; that we might be made the righteousness of God in him.

BIBLE BACKGROUND

The second letter written by Paul to the Corinthians is one of the most personal of all of Paul's writings. Second Corinthians gives us a wealth of information about Paul's movements, experiences, and states of mind during a period that Luke (the author of Acts) passes over almost without comment (Acts 20:1-3). The letter is rich and varied in content, and it reveals much about Paul's character. In Second Corinthians, Paul deals with crises that have arisen in the Corinthian church. His confrontations with these problems caused him to reflect deeply on his relationship with the community and to speak frankly about it. One moment he was venting his feelings of frustration and uncertainty, the next he was pouring out his feelings of relief and affection.

While Paul is confident that his aims and motives are manifest to God, the situation at Corinth is not fully predictable. His primary concern is that the Corinthians recognize the sober, straightforward way he deals with the misunderstandings which have arisen among them. His actions do not seek personal advantage but the church's good.

POINTS TO PONDER

1. *What did Paul mean when he used the phrase, "the terror of the Lord"? (2 Corinthians 5:11)*

2. *Why did Paul take an opportunity to boast? (vv. 13-15)*

3. *Explain what Paul meant when he said, "Wherefore henceforth know we no man after the flesh...." (v. 16)*

4. *What does it mean to be "in Christ"? (v. 17)*

5. *What has God done to provide atonement for our sins? (vv. 18-19)*

6. *To whom did God impute our trespasses? Why? (vv. 20-21)*

LESSON AT-A-GLANCE

1. *Paul encourages reverence (2 Corinthians 5:11-15)*
2. *Paul encourages growth (vv. 16-17)*
3. *Paul encourages reconciliation (vv. 18-21)*

EXPLORING THE MEANING

1. Paul encourages reverence (2 Corinthians 5:11-15)

Paul had just spoken of standing at the judgment of Christ in the previous verses. In the light of the "judgment seat" of Christ, Paul lives and preaches the importance of Christians living in the "fear and admonition" of God. The fear of the Lord, Paul teaches, is not being frightened of the Lord, but it is an attitude of reverence.

In addition to Paul's discourse on fear, he is trying to persuade the Corinthians of his own sincerity. He has no doubt whatsoever that in the sight of God his hands are clean and his motives pure. But his enemies have cast suspicion on them, and he wishes to demonstrate his sincerity to his Corinthian friends. This is not a selfish desire to vindicate himself. Paul's love for God causes him to bring the Gospel message to the Corinthians. "The love of Christ constraineth us" (v. 14). This phrase is sometimes misunderstood. The thought has been that the love of Christ restricts us or straps us down. This is not Paul's meaning. He is saying it is the love of Christ that is motivating us to give out the Word of God.

The love of God constrains us to be obedient to the will of God. Christ died for us; He took our place. Therefore, we should not live for ourselves, but for Him who died for us, and rose again (v. 15, paraphrased). Christ died, not only that we should be delivered from death and judgment, but also that we should be brought up from our state of death into newness of life. Now our lives should be devoted to Him.

2. Paul encourages growth (vv. 16-17)

Paul's outlook has been transformed and made new by his being in Christ. He says, "From now on we regard no one after the flesh; even if we once knew Christ according to the flesh, yet we know Him no longer" (v. 16, NASB). Before Paul's conversion, he regarded all people, including Jesus, after the flesh. He viewed the traditions of Jesus' teaching and claims as blasphemous, and the cross as a shameful thing, God's curse (see Galatians 1:13-14; 3:13b). He judged Christ by human standards and had set out to obliterate the early Christians and eliminate the Christian faith from the world. But Paul changed, and as a result of his conversion and God's redirection of his life, Paul became one of the Lord's greatest missionaries.

Paul affirms that he is now unable to judge anyone from a human point of view. He no longer judges things by the standards of the world's criteria. Similarly, earthly accomplishments cannot become the basis for our Christian valuation, and should not be allowed to affect our attitude toward others or our relationship with one another as children of God.

3. Paul encourages reconciliation (vv. 18-21)

In the beginning, all things were brought into being by the Word of God. So also throughout creation God, through His Son, is the Author of all things. By sin, we set ourselves in rebellion against God; we became enemies of God, alienated from the commonwealth of God.

The sinful nature of humankind revolted against God the Creator. It was not a question of some minor misunderstanding which could easily be put right; it was a case of mutiny, and mutiny of a kind far more radical in its nature and effect than anything that was known in purely human relationships. For the essence of sin is seen in the desire of the creature to set himself in place of the Creator. The wish of sinful human nature is to be God. Because of our rebellion, we became enemies of God and fell out of fellowship with Him. But God "reconciled us to himself" (v. 18). "Reconciled" is one of the most important words in this verse. God is the initiator and goal of reconciliation. Reconciliation proceeds from God and returns to God. Reconciliation is where the rebellion of humankind is matched by the love of God in Christ Jesus.

Those of us who trust Jesus Christ as our Saviour will never have our sins held against us again. Through Jesus Christ, God's holy and loving work of reconciliation has been accomplished once and for all. Now the ministry of reconciliation has been committed by God to His servants. There is no service more crucial and urgent than the exercise of this ministry. God's love for us through Jesus Christ reconciled us back to Himself, and now with His Word, we must reconcile others.

Through the work of the Cross, Jesus Christ has brought humankind and God together again. God has reconciled and has turned His face in love toward the lost world. God does not have to be reconciled to us, because that was accomplished by Christ on the Cross. It is for those of us who are sinners to be reconciled to God. "Religion" is our feeble effort to be reconciled to God. The person who reconciles us to God is Jesus Christ, and the place where we are reconciled is at His Cross.

The result? Because we have trusted Christ as our Saviour, the penalty for all of our sins has been paid and God no longer holds them against us. God has put to our account the very righteousness of Christ. For He made Christ to be sin for us, who knew no sin, that we might be made the righteousness of God in Him.

Through Christ, we are forgiven. Now God can hold out His arms and invite us into fellowship with Him. All God is asking us to do is come to Him. God will not try to get even with us. He doesn't want to punish us. God loves us and wants to restore us to a right relationship with Him through Jesus Christ. Then as Christians, He wants us simply to tell others outside of the body of Christ to be reconciled to Him.

Satan is seeking to tear things apart (John 10:10), but Christ and His Church are involved in the ministry of reconciliation, bringing people back to God and to each other.

DISCERNING MY DUTY

1. *What did Paul mean by his statement "We are known also to your conscience?"*
2. *Why is the flesh (our human nature) a deadly enemy to God?*
3. *Why did Paul say he was "beside" himself? (v. 13)*
4. *Discuss Paul's statement, "Those who live, should live no longer for themselves but for him who died for them and was raised again" (v. 15, NIV).*
5. *How does the doctrine of reconciliation motivate us to serve Christ?*

DECIDING MY RESPONSE

Many in our society today have become disenchanted with the church and have walked away. Many are unsettled by the negative behavior in society and have lost their way. Discuss specific ways that believers can help facilitate the reconciliation of such persons to God and the church. What ways can you help people come to Christ?

As believers, we are ambassadors for God in the world today. This week as an ambassador, minister to someone who is troubled by the unrest of our society by sharing with them the Gospel, the message of reconciliation. Let them know they can have peace and true fellowship with God now by trusting Jesus Christ as their Saviour.

LIGHT ON THE HEAVY

Ambassador. An ambassador is a minister of foreign government or sovereign of the highest rank. When a government sends an ambassador to another government, it means they are on friendly relations. God still loves the world and the believers in Christ are His ambassadors. Believers are citizens of heaven sent into the world as God's ambassadors here on earth.

MORE LIGHT ON THE TEXT

The second Epistle of Paul the apostle to the Corinthians was written as a result of some problems within the church, including a challenge to his apostleship and his authority. The challenge to his apostolic credentials is evident in the chapters 10-13, but the theme of vindication to his ministry is apparent in the first nine chapters. In chapter 4, Paul discusses the theme of his ministry, which he says is Christ (vv. 1-7). He talks about the sufferings and trials that are prevalent in his ministry (vv. 8-15) and the things that motivate him to go on, in spite of his sufferings. These motives include the reward he looks forward to at the judgment, the wonder of being in Jesus' presence forever (5:1-10), the love of Christ demonstrated by His death (vv. 11-16), and the message of reconciliation with which he has been entrusted (vv. 17-21).

2 Corinthians 5:11 Knowing therefore the terror of the Lord, we persuade men; but we are made manifest unto God; and I trust also are made manifest in your consciences.

Verse 11 is connected with the previous thought in verse 10 which talks about standing in the presence of the Lord for judgment when each person will receive what he or she is due from God, because of what has been done in the body, "whether it be good or bad." "The terror of the Lord," refers to the fear of the Lord, from the Greek word *phobos*, which means reverence, awe, or that which causes fear. The word *phobos* is translated "fear" 39 times in the New Testament, and as "terror" three times, including Romans 13:3; 1 Peter 3:14, KJV. The knowledge that he would stand before the throne of God to give account of himself prompts Paul to persuade men.

What did Paul mean by the fear (or terror) of the Lord? At first glance at the sentence, one might be tempted to interpret it as the terror and harshness of God's anger in punishing evil or the terror that the all-powerful God stirs up in the hearts of men (see Genesis 35:5). This is the idea of being afraid of God's anger. Such interpretation would only take into consideration the negative side of the reward or judgment of 2 Corinthians 5:10. Neglecting the positive rewards, which occupied Paul's mind and the greater part of the argument (4:13-5:10), would be out of place. These rewards motivated Paul to continue in ministry in spite of his trials and sufferings (4:8-12). The suggestion, therefore, is to be cognizant of the fact that Paul's sufferings and his reverence for the Lord as his divine assessor, to whom he stands accountable, spurred him to "persuade men."

Such knowledge that "the Lord is to be feared" constitutes one of the most powerful reasons for Paul's zeal to persuade people to be reconciled to God. To "persuade" is the Greek word *peitho*, meaning to convince by argument. What did Paul and others (either other apostles or workers with Paul) try to convince the people about? They were trying to convince them of the authenticity of their ministry and the truth of the Gospel. Paul told them that his motives were pure (1:12), and his credentials and conduct as an apostle were sound (3:1-6; 4:1-6). Paul's goal was also to persuade them of his integrity, and the integrity of the Gospel. Paul declared that the Lord knew him (and his intention to spread the Gospel), i.e., they "are made manifest unto God." To manifest (Greek *phaneroo*) is to make plain or apparent. Paul's conduct, motive, and apostleship for ministry are made plain before God. However, he thought it was necessary that the Corinthians also understand his apostolic status and conduct. "I hope it is also made plain to your conscience." Paul's aim was to commend himself to everyone's conscience (see 4:2). He tried to convey a similar thought in this passage. Paul called their own conscience as their witness.

12 For we commend not ourselves again unto you, but give you occasion to glory on our behalf, that ye may have somewhat to answer them which glory in appearance, and not in heart. 13 For whether we be beside ourselves, it is to God: or whether we be sober, it is for your cause.

Paul insisted that none of the things he had been saying were aimed at recommending himself again (3:1) or soliciting their praise. Rather, his instruction was intended for two things. First, it was intended to be a source of joy and pride for them (i.e., the Corinthians); they were the testimony of Paul and his other workers (3:2). Second, it was intended to be ammunition with which to defend his apostleship against those who took pride in outward appearance, rather than purity of the heart. These were the people who seemed to make a superficial claim of superiority over Paul in their relation to Jesus (5:16) and to the Jewish orthodoxy (11:22). They claimed to have a greater revelation and vision than Paul (12:1- 7). Their aim was to discredit Paul and his co-workers. Paul told the Corinthians that they knew him better. He was not commending himself again, but reminding them once more that they could take pride and be able to defend him and the genuineness and zeal of his ministry.

Paul goes on in verse 13 to defend the rationale of his zeal for the Gospel, and its purpose, "It is to God." This verse is difficult to explain, and a number of proposals have been given by different scholars for its explanation. First, it is proposed that Paul's critics had accused him of being "out of his mind" because of his alleged esoteric teaching (Acts 26:24ff), his rapturous experiences, and his tireless work. A second suggestion is that Paul is referring to his experience of Greek *glossolalia*, i.e., speaking in tongues and visions (Acts. 22:17-21), which led some to say he was "beside himself." His only answer was, "It is for God" or "It is between God and me" (compare 1 Corinthians 14:1). The third proposal is that, on occasion, the Corinthians had viewed Paul as having been carried away by excessive emotion. A fourth proposal is that his self-commendation is a sign of lunacy. The final suggestion is that, in Jewish eyes, Paul's conversion experience on the Damascus road is evidence of his madness. To all of these accusations, Paul says, "If I am mad or not, it is to God," i.e., "for God's glory." However, he says if "we are sober, it is for your cause." The word "sober," which is in Greek *sophroneo*, means to be of sound mind or right mind (compare Mark 5:15; Luke 8:35; Romans 12:3; Titus 2:6; 1 Peter 4:7). To sum up, Paul's thoughts were that it did not matter what the accusation was, it was for the glory of God. We are in our right mind; we are just carrying out the work of God. It is for your own good and benefit that we do what we do.

14 For the love of Christ constraineth us; because we thus judge, that if one died for all, then were all dead: 15 and that he died for all, that they which live should not henceforth live unto themselves, but unto him which died for them, and rose again.

In verses 14 and 15, Paul stated clearly that it was the love of Christ, demonstrated by His death and resurrection that motivated or compelled them to serve Christ and the Corinthians. Paul was stretching the answer he gave in verse 13b by denying the accusation that he and the other workers were mad. He said, in effect, that, no, they were not out of their minds. But when they realized the love of Christ for them through His supreme sacrifice, the joy of it made them behave as if they were mad. The thought of it also constrained them to persuade men to accept the Lord (v. 11). The word "constrain," (Greek *sunecho*), is translated to urge; to press (Acts 18:5), and to throng (Luke 8:45).

Paul attributes the love of Christ as the compelling force for his ministry and conduct. The same Greek verb is used in Luke 12:50 about the compulsion Jesus felt to accomplish His mission. Paul describes how this urge is built up in him. It is based on the conviction that since, "One died for all, then were all dead," then all should "no longer live for themselves, but for him who died for them and was raised again" (NIV). Paul gives two motives (in this isolated passage vv. 11-21) for his Christian service. The first is the knowledge of accountability to Christ (v. 11), and the second is the love of Christ shown by His death.

Paul argues that since one man died both on behalf of and in the place of all men, all men must die (v. 14b). The death he means is the death to sin and self, which is living a Christian life. Although Christ's death offers salvation for all, only those who respond through repentance can appropriate the benefits of His sacrifice. Paul further argues (v. 15) that those who have been saved through Christ should live for Him and "no longer live for themselves." (NIV) They are no longer their own; they belong to Christ (compare 1 Corinthians 6:19) who not only died, but also rose again.

The New Testament always links the death and resurrection of Christ, because the resurrection of Christ proves that He is indeed the author of our salvation. Writing to the Romans, Paul says, that as Christ was raised, so are we raised with Him into a new life (Romans 6:4; 7:6; Colossians 3:1, 2, 10). We are set free from slavery to sin and self into a life of devotion and service to Christ (Romans 6:6-11). The awareness of this fact left Paul with no option but to expend himself in serving Christ through his service to others (2 Corinthians 4:11-12; 12:15; compare Philippians 2:17; 1 Thessalonians 2:8).

16 Wherefore henceforth know we no man after the flesh: yea, though we have known Christ after the flesh, yet now henceforth know we him no more. 17 Therefore if any man be in Christ, he is a new creature: old things are passed away; behold, all things are become new.

The new life in Christ which Paul has experienced has transformed him, given him a new perspective in the way he views man and Christ, and changed him into a new creature. He no longer regards (man and especially Christ) with a worldly perception, but with a spiritual understanding. With the use of the Greek conjunction *hoste* (so or therefore) in verses 16 and 17, the apostle introduces the changes that the death and the resurrection of Christ and a union with the Lord make in people's lives. Because of the death of Christ and the change within Paul himself, he ceased to judge people from a humanistic or "worldly point of view." He no longer based his judgment on the external appearance, but on the heart (v. 12). His prejudiced views based on race and nationality had changed. He now regarded individuals of all races and nationalities primarily in terms of their spiritual status, rather than their nationality. The Jew-Gentile division no longer influenced his life and conduct. What mattered now for Paul was the new relationship with Christ he enjoyed (see Romans 2:28-29; 1 Corinthians 5:12-13; Galatians 3:28; 6:10; Ephesians 2:11-22, etc.). That is why he boldly wrote to the Galatian churches:

"You are all sons (and daughters) of God through faith in Christ Jesus, for all of you who were baptized into Christ have clothed yourselves with Christ. There is neither Jew nor Greek, slave nor free, male nor female, for you are all one in Christ Jesus. If (since) you belong to Christ, then you are Abraham's seed, and heirs according to the promise" (Galatians 3:26-29).

This also changed his earlier sincere, but erroneous, perception of Christ as merely a Messianic pretender, whose followers must be exterminated (see Acts 9:1-2; 26:9-11). Paul had come to recognize Jesus as the promised Messiah whose death had brought life (vv. 14, 15). He did not see Christ as a mere human. His encounter with Jesus on the Damascus road brought a new awareness of who He really is: the Messiah and the Lord God. His relationship with Jesus as Saviour and Lord created an understanding that all believers are brothers and sisters in Christ. His experience with Christ affected his total outlook in life, his goals, and his aspirations. He was no longer guided by fleshly desire, but by the Spirit (see Philippians 3:1-10).

All of these changes in perception and in lifestyle, are the effects of Paul's new relationship with Christ. Paul then makes a very categorical statement, "if any man be in Christ" (v. 17). When anyone accepts Christ by faith he becomes a new creature, i.e., he is recreated. There is a radical change which occurs when one becomes a believer, not a physical or an outward change, but an internal change. The new creation involves new principles of living, new moral ideas, and a new way of thinking. Becoming new in Christ also changes our relationship with people and our attitudes toward life and living. This is the work of the Holy Spirit, and it is consistent with the Lord's teaching when He told Nicodemus that he must be born again in order to enter the kingdom of God (see John 3:5-7). When we become new creatures, "old things pass away."

What are the old things that pass away? Paul gives a long list of things that can be summed up as the old man, or old nature, and are characterized by all types of sin and sinful desires, that must be eradicated (see Romans 6:6-11; Ephesians 4:22; Colossians 3:9). "Behold, all things are become new" added emphasis to the already stated fact. Following the original Greek, "behold" can be interpreted as "indeed" all things have become new.

It is amazing to read the writings of Paul where he talks about the great change that took place when he became a believer in Christ. Reading his short biography in Acts and some bits and pieces of his autobiography (compare Philippians 3:1-11), one is left with wonder and awe at what an encounter with the Lord is able to accomplish in a man like Paul. Paul's change in attitude and perception of man (v. 16) is one of the most radical.

This is a difficult area to deal with in the church today: accepting all people equally, as children of God. Race is still a big problem in our churches. The old problem of discrimination, for which Paul challenged Peter and his fellow apostles, is still apparent in churches today. If you are Black, you automatically are expected to belong to a Black church; and if you are a Black pastor it is assumed that you have no place in a White congregation. The Chinese, the Native Americans, and many other groups of people have formed separate churches, not for the purpose of spreading the Gospel, but for human and self-preservation. Many White Christians still regard Christians of other races as inferior. The truthful statement, "We are all one in Christ" is used only as a cliché, and no one seems to mean it. The song, "We Are One in the Bond of Love" often does not include other races in our midst and is sung without serious consideration of its meaning.

18 and all things are of God, who hath reconciled us to himself by Jesus Christ, and hath given us the ministry of reconciliation; 19 To wit, that God was in Christ, reconciling the world unto himself, not imputing their trespasses unto them; and hath committed unto us the word of reconciliation.

"All this is from God" (NIV) refers to the new attitude and perception in life (v. 18), as well as the new creation (v. 17). Paul attributes the changes that take place in man to God. God is the Author of the second creation, just as He is of the first (compare 4:6). This new creation is what Paul calls the work of grace (see Ephesians 2:8-10). "All things are of God" takes away any notion that salvation can be earned or achieved through human effort and nullifies the humanistic world-view that says man's destiny is within himself. Paul explains this new creation, which is the result of our new relationship to God accomplished in Christ's death and resurrection, as the process of reconciliation. God initiates the process and carries out the work of reconciliation between man and Himself. Again, it is all God, without man's effort or contribution. The phrase, "by (i.e., through) Jesus Christ" means that Christ is the medium through whom the reconciliation is accomplished.

The verb "reconciled" is translated from the Greek verb *katallasso*, meaning to change mutually, and from the noun katallage, meaning exchange, or restoration to (the divine) favor, atonement, reconciliation. It has the idea of re-establishing a broken relationship between enemies, making peace between two or more opposing parties. In estranged or broken relationships, people sometimes settle their differences alone or they involve a third party. The third party could be the judge or an arbitrator in a court of law. God is both the plaintiff who was offended and the arbitrator and judge. Man is the offender. Although man cannot erase his sin, God decides to reconcile with man. God did this by sending His Son to die on behalf of man to purchase man's redemption.

The concept of reconciliation is very important in the Pauline epistles and seems to be equivalent with justification. Both words appear as parallels in much of Paul's writings. For example, in Romans 5:9-11, Paul writes:

"Since we have now been justified by his blood, how much more shall we be saved from God's wrath through him. For if, when we were God's enemies, we were reconciled to him through the death of his Son, how much more, having been reconciled, shall we be saved through his life. Not only is this so, but we also rejoice in God through our Lord Jesus Christ, through whom we have received reconciliation" (NIV).

The emphasis in the passage, however, is on the love of God rather than His wrath (see Romans 5:8). Therefore, reconciliation, which is based on the love of God, constitutes the foundation for the new creation, in which old things pass away and all things become new (v. 17). Being reconciled with God is removing that which stands in the way of a right relationship between God and man, i.e., re-establishing or restoring the broken relationship caused by sin in the garden of Eden (see Isaiah 59:2).

Continuing this concept, Paul adds that God also "hath given us the ministry of reconciliation" (2 Corinthians 5:18). Not only has our relationship with God been restored, but we have also been given the ministry to bring about reconciliation to the world—to those not yet reconciled. Although Paul was referring to himself and his fellow workers, this ministry is also true for all believers. We are now God's agents of reconciliation, and as Paul calls us, God's "ambassadors" (v. 20).

Verse 19 emphasizes the concept and explains the process further. The statement, "To wit (meaning or namely) that was in Christ, reconciling the world unto himself," reinforces a fact already established in the previous verse: God is the one who does the reconciling. Repeating it here serves as emphasis. Although it is all God, God uses man as an instrument to spread "the word of reconciliation." Paul also reiterates in strong terms that all this is done through Christ.

How does God reconcile believers to Himself? The answer is clear, by "not imputing their trespasses unto them." The word, imputing (Greek *logizomai*) means to take an inventory; to reckon or count; to put down into one's account. Paul said that in the process of reconciliation, God does not allow man's sinful nature to stand in the way of His desire to mend the broken relationship between Himself and the world. Although God knows that the world offends Him through disobedience and rejection, because of His love He offers forgiveness anyway. Paul seemed to say: God offers forgiveness to all by giving His Son as a ransom (see Matthew 20:28, Hebrews 9:15). Because of His love God "hath committed unto us the word (message) of reconciliation." That message is the same as Christ's commission to His disciples (see Matthew 28:18-20; Mark 16:15-20; Acts 1:8) to proclaim the Good News about reconciliation.

20 Now then we are ambassadors for Christ, as though God did beseech you by us: we pray you in Christ's stead, be ye reconciled to God. 21 For he hath made him to be sin for us, who knew no sin; that we might be made the righteousness of God in him.

As proclaimers of the good tidings of the "Gospel of peace" (Ephesians 6:15), Paul said, "now then (therefore) we are ambassadors (Greek *presbeuo*) for Christ." That means we are duly appointed and official messengers or representatives of Christ, acting on His behalf. It is as if God Himself were pleading to others through us (by our preaching) to receive the offer of reconciliation given through Christ's death. Paul offered a direct invitation to the people to accept the offer. Using another word for plea, "we pray you," that is, "we implore or beg you," Paul exhorted the readers to allow the reconciliation God offers to take effect in them. This is a call for response from man. The offer is there, but it must be appropriated by a positive response to be effective. Using the concept of banking, the check has been issued by God to everyone, it is left to each recipient to cash it in, in order to receive the benefit.

Verse 21 poses some difficulties in its interpretation. The difficulties lie mainly in the first part of the verse. What does Paul mean by the statement "for he hath made him to be sin?" A number of suggestions have been given to disentangle the puzzle. They include, first, that Christ was treated as if He were a sinner, by becoming the object of God's wrath and bore the penalty and guilt of sin. This matches in some measure Paul's statement to the Galatians (3:13), "Christ redeemed us from the curse of the law, having become a curse for us." This is an allusion based on the Old Testament Law that pronounced a curse to anyone who did not abide by all that was written in the Law (see Deuteronomy 27:26; compare 21:23). This has the idea of substitution.

The second suggestion has the notion that in His incarnation, Christ took on the human nature "in the likeness of sinful flesh" (see Romans 8:3). God made Him to be sin, thus, participation. The third concept deals with His becoming a sacrifice for sin (i.e., sin offering). Christ was made to be sin, an Old Testament concept of sacrifice. By paying the penalty for our sin with His death on the Cross, and by being born as a man and tempted as we are tempted, Christ identified with the human sinful nature, and took on Himself the consequences of sin on behalf of mankind. The sinlessness of Christ is echoed in Peter's statement, where he quoted Isaiah's prophecy (see 1 Peter 2:22; compare Isaiah 53:9).

The last part of this verse (v. 21) declares God's intent for making Christ "to be sin." That is, "that we might be made the righteousness of God in him." This is a mystery and is the Good News for all. God, through His Love, laid on Christ the iniquity of us all (see Isaiah 53:6) so "that we might be made the righteousness of God, in Christ." Through Christ, man's sins are forgiven, and man can become righteousness before God. "Righteousness" (Greek *dikaiosune*) means to have a right standing before God, which is also translated as justification. Jesus took our sin and in exchange gave us His righteousness. Based on Christ's sacrificial death, God declares the believer justified or righteous in his sight. This mystery, together with the knowledge of the fear of God (v. 11), the love of Christ (v. 14), and the message of reconciliation, motivated Paul and his fellow workers to continue in the ministry, in spite of all hardships (4:8ff). This truth should also motivate us in our own Christian walk.

ABOUT THE AUTHOR

Dr. Melvin E. Banks is the founder of Urban Ministries, Inc., the largest African-American Christian media and content provider, serving over 50,000 churches with curriculum, books, magazines, Bible studies, videos, teaching resources, and more.

Alabama native Dr. Banks began his spiritual journey at the age of 12, sharing Bible stories with younger children and traveling with his mentor to Birmingham's remote parts to give his testimony to adults. Inspired by Hosea 4:6, where God says, "My people are destroyed from lack of knowledge," he established UMI in 1970 to publish positive images of African-Americans in the biblical experience. During its first 12 years, UMI operated from the basement of the Banks' home, and Dr. Banks marketed his first Sunday School curriculum, *InTeen*, to churches out of his car's trunk.

Dr. Banks received an honorary doctorate from his alma mater, Wheaton College, where he served as a trustee for many years. Moody Bible Institute honored him as an Alumnus of the year, and Dr. Banks was recognized for his achievements by the History Makers Foundation.

Today UMI's innovative work has led to many publishers becoming more ethnically and racially diverse in their efforts. Materials include Sunday School curriculum, Vacation Bible School resources, books, videos, music, and website UrbanFaith.com – all of which speak to people of color in the context of their culture. For more information, please visit: UrbanMinistries.com.

www.ingramcontent.com/pod-product-compliance
Lightning Source LLC
Chambersburg PA
CBHW032034290426
44110CB00012B/801